Call Me
JONAH

By Will Alexander

For permission, serialization, condensation, adaptations, or for our catalog of other publications, write to Ozark Mountain Publishing, Inc., P.O. Box 754, Huntsville, AR 72740, ATTN: Permissions Department.

Library of Congress Cataloging-in-Publication Data

Call Me Jonah

by Will Alexander -1961-

Call Me Jonah is the story of an ordinary man who experiences such extraordinary moments starting in childhood and that continue throughout his lifetime.

1. (NED) Near Death Experience 2. Spirit World 3. Metaphysical

I. Alexander, Will -1961- II. (NED) Near Death Experience   III. Metaphysical   IV. Title

Library of Congress Catalog Card Number: 2023936086

ISBN: 978-1-950639-20-5

Cover Art and Layout: Victoria Cooper Art
Book set in: Times New Roman
Book Design: Summer Garr
Published by:

PO Box 754, Huntsville, AR 72740
800-935-0045 or 479-738-2348; fax 479-738-2448
WWW.OZARKMT.COM

Printed in the United States of America

To L., the great love of my life

Contents

Prologue

When I was a boy, there came a day that I should have died. Odd as this sounds, I consider myself lucky because of it. My brush with mortality must have been fated, because it opened a door to another world that has never closed and my childhood ended long ago.

Here's the thing about doors—not only do they let what's inside a space out, but they also let what's on the outside *in*. It's this flow between sides which lends something extraordinary to this story. Throughout my life, interactions with another, *higher* world have continued.

Trust me, I know how peculiar it sounds. It doesn't alter the fact that it's true. I first met Someone from that other side when I was dying. Obviously, I didn't die. Yet what happened during the incident affected everything to come afterward. The care this presence gave me during my direst moments was beyond anything I have experienced since. Though decades ago, my heart still sings from the encounter as if it happened yesterday.

Which is what made things so confusing when the child I was then tried to tell my parents what happened. Without understanding why, I immediately saw how uncomfortable my talk of it, *of her*, made them. On the spot, I decided never to bring it up again. I haven't.

One trip into the mystical could be explained away as an isolated, trauma-induced event. Little did I know that Someone else would come, and others after that at unexpected moments. Strangely, they were intimately familiar and yet, at the same time, utterly removed. Each left me something priceless. Always, too, when it was most desperately needed.

Until now, I kept the vow of silence that I once took. It should never be easy to gush about the sacred moments in your life. They're too precious to give away cheaply. What changed is me. I started to reconsider as a man the choice I made as a boy to keep my story hidden.

While I deliberated, another interloper entered the scene, telling me to tell this story. The other siders achieve what they set out to do, especially once you learn that their wisdom is inescapable. Conceding this, maybe it's time I yielded to them.

This whole thing began when I was little …

CHAPTER 1
LIZABETH

My birthday was a week away. I'd be turning nine. And, coolest thing, it would happen while we were away on a trip.

Up front in the driver's seat, Dad yawned. He stretched his arm, said he was tired and that he felt like stopping for the night. Sitting next to him, Mom said she did too. My two sisters and me itched to get out of the car. Our family was going down to our grandparents' house in Florida during Easter break. We lived up in Ohio by a great lake. Mom told us it'd be a really long drive down there. She wasn't kidding. My butt felt numb from sitting. I didn't know how long we'd been in the car, but it seemed like forever.

Thinking about what'd happen once we got there was exciting. Where they lived was tropical. They had a swimming pool! Palm trees grew in their front yard and in the back they had orange trees. When the oranges got ripe, Grams picked them and made a jelly she called marmalade that my sisters and I loved. Before every Christmas, a package of it got delivered to our house that we waited for all winter. Mom called it Sunshine in a Jar. She

1

would let us open a jar at breakfast on Christmas morning before church. Kind of a family tradition.

Anyway, it was getting dark when we pulled off the highway. I asked where we were and was told not far from the Tennessee state line. Well, where were we now, then? Still in Kentucky, my dad said. Just ahead, Mom saw a Holiday Inn right off the highway and said we should stay there. She told Dad that we oughta stick with a chain because they had nicer rooms than the mom-and-pop places.

Before checking in, we drove through McDonald's to get something to eat. This was smart, because my sisters and I had been complaining about how hungry we were. It took a while to get our order, though. My older sister special ordered her hamburger without the onions they put on it. Or else she freaked out. This always slowed things down. Mickey D's wasn't too fast with special orders, but our food finally came. Not long after wolfing down burgers and fries, we got to the motel and into a room with two big beds. Mom and Dad got one, Kris and Kara got the other one. Of course, being the only boy, they'd give me the lumpy-looking cot a worker rolled in. It was the same whenever we took trips.

While my sisters played with dolls on top of their bed, I finished the last of a small stack of comic books. Superman saved the world by spinning the Earth backward then going back in time to stop the bad guy from messing things up there. The world was saved again. Good, but the Man of Steel did the same thing in every comic. Bored, I tossed this book along with the others on the cot and stared at the fan on the wall making a big racket. Mom noticed. She told Dad that after sitting for seven hours in the car, the kids needed to burn off some energy or they'd never sleep tonight. How would he feel about taking us to the pool?

My ears perked up. Living up north, summers seemed short and not hot enough to give us many good days for swimming. The idea of us kids ending our first day on the road at a pool sounded like a dream come true. We had seen it glittering there, a huge glass dome, at the end of the motel when Dad went to pay for the room. "Yes!" I shouted at Mom's idea. So did my sisters, who'd been arguing about whose doll had on a better outfit but suddenly figured out what Mom and Dad were talking about. "Can we? Please!" Kara and Kris chimed in.

Mom laughed and told us to get our bathing suits on.

* * *

"Tommy, don't hang out there by yourself on that side. It's too deep. Go over to the steps where your sisters are playing." Dad pointed to them. It was a rectangular pool. We had been there for just a few minutes. He and my mother were leaning back on chairs around the middle part. Kara and Kris splashed around at the shallow end.

Standing on the far side, I looked down at the *9 Feet* sign painted on the pool edge by my feet. I could handle it. Dad should know that about me. Inside the dome, the air was thick. The glass on the upper part of the dome was covered with steam. Smells from the chemicals they put in to keep the water clean was strong and I didn't like it. Still, it was a pool and a thing we didn't get a crack at every day. No way I wasn't going to use it. Besides, other than us, no one else was there.

Dad watched and waved me back toward him. I tried to listen to everything he said. He was my hero and I wanted to be like him. He always made time for me. When he wasn't at the office, he helped with my homework if I got stuck. We built things together.

He liked sci-fi television shows and explained their ideas until I started to like them. Even though he was too busy at work to coach my little league team like some of my friends' fathers, he'd take me to the baseball diamond on Saturday mornings during the spring so I could practice hitting and pitching. The two of us spent hours there. Baseball was our thing. So when he told me to stay away from the deep end, I sulked back to where he and Mom sat. When I was maybe halfway there, they stopped staring at me. Hmm. This might be my chance.

It wasn't that I wanted to disobey him. Only impress him. I wasn't that young anymore, plus I swam good enough, sort of. Dad talked about growing up in Michigan on a street that ended at the shore of a lake. His stories about ice skating in the winter, sailing a skiff in the spring, and then—he smiled most remembering this—whole summers swimming with his brothers when school was out—made me glad for him. And a little jealous too. Dad having this dream life when he was growing up musta' been great. But I didn't have any brothers. No boys to skate with, sail with, or accept a dare to swim to the bottom of a lake and prove it by bringing up a stone or stick. Like he was lucky enough to do when he was a kid.

Okay, even if I didn't grow up around water year round, I would show him. I was bigger than average for my age, decent at sports, ran faster than any other boy in my grade, and was pretty strong. How hard could it be to swim down to the bottom of this pool, touch the drain, then pop back up and brag about what I just did? Dad would think it was pretty cool.

I walked right on past him and my mother, then my sisters flicking water at each other on the steps and kept right on going around the pool until I stopped where I began at the *9 Feet* marker. No one was watching anymore. Go time. Holding onto the edge, I slipped my legs into the water without making a sound. Then the rest of me. My plan was working.

I was doing it! Not wanting them to notice me yet, I moved my arms and legs but only under the surface. It didn't take long for me to see that barely moving like this wasn't enough to keep me from sinking.

Already, I sucked in a little water between kicks when my body sank lower. Still trying to be quiet, I thrashed around even harder below the surface. But it wasn't enough to keep my head out. I swallowed more water. The chemical taste was awful. Making things worse, I'd pushed out pretty far from the edge. Thinking about how deep the water under me was, the gap seemed like a mile.

Aw, man, I was in trouble. Dad would be mad I hadn't listened but there wasn't any choice but to get his help. About to yell for him, I gulped in more water and only got out a cough. My younger sister Kara heard it, though. She turned to see me, then said to Kris, "Look at Tommy showing off down there after Dad told him to stay out. He's gonna get in trouble!" They shrugged at each other and starting playing again. My parents were still talking and didn't see me fighting not to go down. Better call out again and fast.

I tried to take a big breath this time before calling for help but my mouth hit the water again and I choked. My head went all the way under. No matter how hard I kicked my legs and fought with my arms, it wasn't making any difference. Pretending to be a good swimmer was a huge mistake.

Right then, something strange happened. I was watching everything happen like in a movie. Sort of in slow-motion too. I saw a boy fighting to swim but getting nowhere. I watched him fighting and knew how mixed up he was not knowing what to do next. But, even weirder, it wasn't *me* now. Somehow, I was outside myself watching this happen. I also felt smarter, or at least like I could understand things better. Then it got even stranger.

You're okay, a voice said. *I'm here with you.* It wasn't actually words this other person said as much as something that came clearly into my head. I looked around but couldn't see anything except for myself sinking further down. My eyes didn't work except to see straight in front. Something thick and gray blocked all side views as well as behind me. To tell the truth, I didn't even know *how* to turn around to see if this person was there. So, I couldn't even see this person talking to me.

Who are you? Who's here with me? I wondered in my head. Then this Someone got a name.

Lizabeth, it answered. *Do you remember? I'm not a stranger to you.* Her name did seem familiar as did the tone of her voice. Somebody, maybe, that I met once but had forgotten until reminded just this minute.

Lizabeth? I thought back, getting the hang of how things worked. It surprised me how easy this was, talking not in words but by thinking them. It made sense, because the other me couldn't have talked even if he wanted to. That little boy was under water, not breathing, and at the pool's bottom.

I've always been with you. Since the before time. She was so calm. *You have nothing to be afraid of, I promise. You will never need to be afraid.* Automatically, I knew every word of this was true. Truer than any promise anyone else had ever made to me.

Even though I couldn't see her, she was hugging me all over. It felt warm and wonderful. I couldn't be safer. Although both of us were in this outside place watching the other me lay on the pool bottom, I wasn't worried or mixed up anymore. Just the opposite, everything made sense, as if I was always meant to be in this moment. Things here were fine. Better than fine. Perfect even. This outside place was totally different but I liked it there.

What's going on? How can I see myself like this? Then an idea came to me, although it clashed with my feeling more alive than ever.

Did I die?

No, you didn't. You aren't going to die today.

Lizabeth loved me intensely. She radiated goodness. I felt inside myself. It was like being hugged by my mother and grandmother at the same time, but stronger still. This was something I noticed right away: her power. It was a shield through which nothing could pass that might hurt me.

I have to go now. You do too. Your family needs you back. But I am always by your side, whether or not you see me. Remember this. Whenever you most need me, I will be there like I am now. She was saying her good-bye. It saddened me that she had to leave. Wait, there was one more thing I needed to ask.

Are you my guardian angel? From Sunday school, I remembered the deacon telling us that everyone had one. The way she protected me, what else could she be? But Lizabeth didn't answer my question. She started pulling away. The warm, safe feeling was ending along with my new understanding. Childhood returned to the way I thought.

Shoot, Lizabeth had gone. I wanted her to stay. What happens to me now? I couldn't stay in this outside place. The other smarter me told me so before going. If you were a living person, it wasn't allowed. So what would come next? I didn't wonder long. Everything went black.

Next thing I knew, Dad was shaking me by the shoulders. After opening my eyes, I saw his worried face. From the water dripping off him, he must have jumped in the pool. I was laying on the side deck, so he rescued me. Mom, also right there, was saying oh my God, oh my God. Kara and Kris stood behind her looking terrified.

Lizabeth was totally gone now. So was the outside place that felt so nice. I could tell because the wet tiles underneath me felt cold on my back. With Lizabeth, everything felt warm. That's how I was sure she had left. Also, I was back inside *me* again.

"Tommy? Hey, he opened his eyes!" Dad shouted. He rolled me over on my side. He must have known what was coming because a minute later I threw up a lot of that gross pool water. Mom was thanking the Lord. Seeing I was okay, my sisters started jumping up and down. "Daddy saved Tommy!" Kris whooped, in between hops.

"Great job, honey!" Mom praised him. "I'm so thankful you remembered some of those lifeguarding skills from growing up on a lake." Dad glanced at her, nodded fast, then looked away. *Don't be thanking me*, he was thinking. He was ashamed about what just happened, that he was so busy with Mom he missed out on what I was doing. He was also thinking, *Good Lord, this could have ended badly*. Being able to do this was all new to me and I wondered why I could suddenly hear what was in his head. Maybe it was still that other me that knew more things than this me. It only lasted for a few minutes, though, then the other me went away like Lizabeth.

Dad checked to see if I was ready to sit up. I said yes but didn't tell him not to be ashamed because I was all right. What he was thinking was private, and it would be wrong to say anything about it. "You gave us a wicked scare, Tommy," he said with his hand still on my shoulder.

"You didn't have a thing to worry about, Dad. I didn't need rescuing," I told him, then looked at Mom. My parents looked at

8

each other and then back again at me. I saw that they definitely didn't get it.

"I was okay the whole time."

"How do you mean?" Mom asked.

"Because Lizabeth was there. She told me I would be fine. I knew she was right."

They looked at each other again. Like what I just said was really creepy. Who is Lizabeth? Dad asked Mom. Don't know, she said back. I never heard Tommy mention that name before. Then Mom came back to me. "Is she an imaginary friend or something?"

"Don't be silly," I answered. "I never had a make-believe friend and I'm not going to start now. *Little kids* have them, not big ones like me." I'd be nine next week, for crying out loud.

I could see their faces, though. For some reason, the talk of Lizabeth really bothered them. So I dropped it. I decided then and there not to talk about her or what happened in front of them. Or anyone else. It would stay just between me and Lizabeth. For many years to come.

* * *

Florida burst with sunshine and we had a fantastic time there. My ninth birthday stood out for being the only one I got to celebrate in a warm place instead of the usual March gloom in Ohio.

Another reason that made it special were the gifts my grandparents gave me. Gramps got me an autographed *Johnny Bench* bat and glove set. The glove I wore out during my little league years. The bat, which I couldn't stand to think of being broken or nicked up, stayed on the shelf in my room with other sports trophies. Grams wasn't crazy about sports, so she gave me a set of illustrated children's encyclopedias. I read them cover to cover so many times—Aardvark to Zulu—the binding fell apart on them. But did I soak up a lot of information!

Lizabeth … well, she never returned the rest of my childhood or during my teens. *Lizabeth*. Who was she really? When I got a little older, it dawned on me that this was probably a name she picked because it rang softly enough in a child's ear. After all, weren't angels supposed to have regal names like Gabriel, Michael, or Uriel? Melodic and male ones that always ended in an *–el,* right? Mine had a folksy, female name. If that's even what she was. Lizabeth never had answered me when I asked about her status. Yet if her name was common enough, there was nothing ordinary about her power. For the rest of my life, whenever I let my mind travel back to this encounter, I remembered every sensation, every insight as if they just occurred.

There were no other lasting effects. I was similar to my friends and shared their interests. Testing our toughness, excelling in sports, discovering girls, and doing well in school took up the bulk of my time. Maybe the only difference was that starting in my teens, I discovered a knack for reading people better. Every now and then and even when I wasn't trying, their thoughts or feelings seemed to swirl more thickly in the air right around me. Sometimes, I tuned into bits and pieces of what they were actually thinking. Not enough to paint a whole picture, yet enough to know what was on their minds.

It was nothing to brag about. Everyone had intuition, didn't they?

CHAPTER 2
PLAINFIELD, OHIO

"It must be him, run, man! There's a car heading over. Here he comes!" Johnny yelled in panic, stepping on the smoldering butt of the joint that he smoked. With his father being a hard-nosed policeman in our town, he had the most to lose if we got busted by the security guard.

"Yeah, he *is* coming!" Nick chimed in.

Mark, the steadiest in our group, piped up. "Time to go. If we get caught or arrested," he said, making eye contact with me, "our parents will disown us." He was the sharpest of our group and with him I could talk over good books, not just sports or girls or the social scene.

"Yeah, but let's go without any drama," I said, aiming these words at ever-nervous Johnny.

Still dripping wet, with clothes hastily thrown on, we abandoned what was left of the Budweiser and bolted for the fence. It was a high one similar to those surrounding home plates at baseball fields. This one protected the country club's swimming pool. It was there to prevent intruders from using the facility after hours. Or bored high-schoolers with nothing better to do on a steamy July night. Our girlfriends, who didn't really care much about us and whom we weren't crazy about either, had ditched us for the movies. Our relationships were more style than any substance. They made us look good and vice versa. Free of them, we decided to have a boys' night out.

By the time the rent-a-cop's car pulled up to the pool's gate, we had already climbed to the top of the fence. At sixteen, we were agile as alley cats. In two blinks of an eye, we scaled down the other side. Now it was the security guard who looked like the one trapped inside a cage. Having dodged the lawman, we laughed as we ran a quarter mile across an open field toward Mark's sports utility vehicle. We'd parked it on a nearby lane without streetlights to better conceal our caper. How clever we were.

Mark and Nick, both over six feet tall, sprinted out in front. I was in the middle, with Johnny bringing up the rear of our pack. I glanced backward to make sure the thick-in-the-middle guard decided not to chase us. His flashlight, swiveling in multiple directions from the same spot, showed he had lost us in the darkness. We pulled it off; what a rush! Looking ahead, I saw my two friends form a single-file line over the last stretch of ground they still needed to cover. It took them far to the left of where our SUV sat. They'd have to backtrack. What were they doing? The shortest distance between two points was a straight line. I veered off and made a beeline toward the SUV. Throwing a glance over my shoulder, I saw that Johnny followed me. As the unofficial leader of the group, I typically set the tone by doing my own thing and letting them decide whether or not to come along. For some reason, they always did.

Mark and Nick reached the curb of the lane fifty yards in front and to my left. Giving us game, they told us to catch up, not knowing we weren't behind them anymore. Got 'em. We'd take the straight line and beat them to the vehicle. Then Johnny and me would flip the script and return their taunts. Running full speed, I was closing fast and guessed about six more strides would seal my triumph. Then five ... four ... Oh my God, *the ditch*! Making a split-second adjustment, I was airborne.

* * *

Plainfield, Ohio. My father got a job offer he couldn't refuse when I was fourteen. So we packed up and moved from the northeastern part of the state to the southwestern part. On a map, it was the opposite side from where we had lived. Turned out that the oppositeness wasn't just geographic. It applied every which way you could imagine. Until then, my early life in Gates Falls had been thoroughly midwestern. According to the local creed, family came first, church second, school third, and country fourth. These values were the bedrock of a heartland upbringing and drummed into me.

And while it happened to be the same state, our family might as well have landed on the moon. Plainfield, nestled between Dayton and Columbus, which Dad chose for its proximity to clients in both, would have made for a good episode of *The Twilight Zone*. Priorities and lifestyles there were so different that it was like my family had been transported to a parallel universe. Few outsiders driving past on Interstate 70 could ever have guessed at the rampant decadence in this plain-looking town.

Socially, Plainfield had two groups, Haves and Could Haves. The Haves consisted of business owners, doctors, bankers, lawyers, and other white-collar types and their families. Because of my father's career as consumer products executive, my mother, sisters, and I rode his coattails into this clique. Mark, who lived around the corner on the swankiest street in the entire city, might as well have been a poster boy for Haves. His father was an oral surgeon, and their family enjoyed the lifestyle that came with it. Unlike some Haves, though, Mark displayed no better-than-everyone-else attitude. Which is why we hit it off so well. He and I knew our fathers were the reason we were Haves, not because of anything we'd done. Most Haves lived atop a ridge on the eastern side of town.

On the western side, in a valley, was the larger Could Haves section of town. Those living there included factory workers, skilled tradesmen, or day laborers along, obviously, with their wives and kids. As owner of a small plumbing company, Nick's father, and therefore Nick, belonged to this group. Athletics tended to be the way for Could Have boys to move up. For girls, beauty, as a passport to social climbing, or eventually marrying up, were the primary paths out. Johnny, whose father had a job as a police officer, was a rare in-betweener. He moved easily among both crowds.

Even so, the Could Haves were hardly lacking. Here, they lived larger than the middle class everywhere else. For one simple reason: Dynotec, a gigantic flooring company. Founded sixty years before, this business exploded when cookie-cutter subdivisions sprang feverishly up on what was once farmland across this region. As it thrived, so did those hired there. It wasn't atypical for people who dropped out of high school to earn incomes rivaling those of professionals in bigger cities. This kind of money and the lifestyle it provided acted like a beacon. Word spread throughout the tri-state area. Whole clans from hamlets in Appalachia flew to Plainfield like moths to a flame. Their menfolk took dirty, dangerous, and yet outlandishly high-paying jobs in the plant. Never minding the formaldehyde smell seeping out of its smokestacks and settling over the valley districts, nor the curiously large number of retirees stricken with cancer. Nothing deterred these country poor searching for their own slice of the good life.

Minus much education, financially clueless, yet loaded with surplus cash, the Dynotec workers spent deliriously. Often times for new Ford F-150s, hulking motor homes, or sparkling speedboats, all perched like trophies in the drives of modest ranch homes. For others, the icing on their cake might be weekend getaway places not far from where they came, near Lake Cumberland or Huntington. Regardless of where they relaxed or how many symbols of excess they acquired, these adults paid little attention to how the newfound wealth affected those around them.

If this was how Could Have grown-ups wasted their good fortune, their kids took things in a more sinister direction. Instead of sports cars or jet skis, they spent just as wantonly—on drugs. Alcohol too, but the preference was drugs due to the variety of highs. Up or down, mellow or jacked, hallucinogenic or body-affecting, teenagers had a range of escapes available just one phone call away.

This explained why any illegal substance you wanted already waited in a bag in someone's locker at my high school. The DEA could have spent a month there cleaning it out. Amphetamines, quaaludes, acid/microdots, weed, hashish, crystal meth, and for those with enough money, the aristocrat of contraband, cocaine. Where it all came from the high school dealers couldn't say. All they knew was their own suppliers never lacked the goods. Nor were there any rules on how old the kid buying needed to be, including fourteen-year-old freshmen. Nobody ever troubled themselves about these sticky moral matters because the flow didn't slow. Any given day, a slew of students got high before homeroom, in their cars at lunch, or after the final bell. With so many using, my school's unusual number of teen pregnancies may have caused confusion among the staff but definitely didn't among us. "Drugs, sex, rock-n-roll," a stupid cliché most places, was a literal way of life here.

If dope didn't happen to be your thing, alcohol was just as easy to obtain. A lot of the town's partying parents provided the booze. To them, it was safer for their kids than dope. Oddly, some found it wildly amusing to see their son or daughter play beer pong with the grown-ups, scarf down jello shots, slur their words, lose their balance, and either pass out or throw up. Guess it struck these parents as old-fashioned fun. Where other grown-ups were who should have known what was happening and stopped it— teachers, counselors, coaches, principals, school nurses, beat cops—my friends and I couldn't figure out.

Regardless of whether you were a Have or a Could Have, the party raged on. It devoured so many kids who didn't have the will power to resist it while mom and dad were off waterskiing for the weekend or on benders themselves at second homes in the hills.

The main difference between these social groups was that the majority who paid the steepest price came from the Could Haves. Not that the Haves were made of any better stuff, because they weren't. It was just that they had stronger family structures which let slide a periodic joint or pilfered oxycodone pill from mom's medicine cabinet, but still drew a sharp line against full-scale addiction. If crossed, a Have kid would end up in a rehabilitation clinic and once out, switched to a Catholic or military school after the family moved to a new city. They had the means to do it.

Sadly, this same boundary line had gaping holes in it among the Could Haves, if it existed at all. Their economic lifeline was

Dynotec and if they cut it by leaving the factory, the only place they could go was back to sad little places in Appalachia. This left their kids much more vulnerable to permanent damage. The smarter, or maybe just the luckier ones from the Could Haves, still had a chance to avoid being stuck the rest of their lives in Plainfield. But it took extraordinary strength to swim against its currents and break free. Few would.

* * *

For a split second, flying through the sticky night air was surreal. Between the beer buzz and adrenalin rush from dodging the law, at least that's how it felt. This sensation didn't last.

Wham! I landed hard on grass and some pebbles, barely clearing the far side of a drainage ditch that paralleled the lane. In my hurry to reach the car before Nick and Mark, I all but forgot what they remembered—the stupid trench. Coming up fast behind me, Johnny did forget. I yelled "Jump!" but he didn't understand in time and fell headlong into it. I heard a thwack when he hit the ground. On doubling back, I saw his shape laying against the up-slope. It was too dark to see his face, but I heard his moaning.

"Holy smokes, Johnny! Are you okay? Toldja to jump! Late, for sure. But I did try."

Completing their detour, Mark and Nick were back at the SUV now. Abandoning all stealth, I shouted at them to hurry over. Johnny needed help. They hustled to my voice and joined me at the edge of the ditch. Each of them grabbed an arm and hoisted him, gently, out. "Be careful, guys," I cautioned, not knowing Johnny's condition.

"Damn!" Nick exclaimed, after seeing how wide the trench was. "Are you all right?"

"Think so. Nothing feels busted," Johnny meekly answered. Probably, he was still too high to tell if anything was broken.

"Good enough for now," I said. "C'mon! Let's get out of here before the real police come." I was genuinely worried his father might show up in a cruiser. "Nick, go ahead and drive. Me and Mark will sit with him in the back to make sure he's all right."

Since it was his car, Mark tossed the keys to Nick, then helped me ease Johnny into the back seat. "Nothing busted on you, right?" Mark asked. He wanted to be sure the only thing hurt on our buddy was his pride.

"Think so," Johnny repeated in a half-whisper.

As Nick started the engine and pulled away from the curb, Dr. Mark Jr., offspring of the town's leading medical professional, emerged as he oftentimes did when one of us took a lick. In the dimness of the car, he commenced his evaluation. "Everything still working like it should?" Johnny stretched out both arms to show they worked okay. Ditto for his legs. "You seem to be fine," Dr. Mark surmised.

"Yeah, except for my right side feels wet. Must have been water in the ditch I didn't notice."

"Let me see that area."

The only light available came from the cones under the streetlamps that we passed on the road. Between this exam and the guilt creeping up on us, we didn't dare flip on the dome light inside the SUV. Instead, Mark and I would get a split second to check, wait until the next cone, then hurry to check again. After a number of these fleeting glimpses, Dr. Mark announced, "I can't be 100% sure in this lighting, but it's not water. The spot on your jeans is way too dark for that. It's blood."

"Can't be. I landed on a grassy slope. There mighta' been a few small stones, but nothing big." Confident in his diagnosis, Dr.

Mark Jr. begged to differ. "Well, one or more of them must have been sharp enough. I'd say you cut yourself somehow. Unbuckle your jeans so I can see your hip."

"Get lost!" But Johnny, in pain, quickly changed his mind and caved in. "It's probably a little gash at most," he predicted.

"Yes, maybe. But quit stalling. Pull down your jeans a little. *Now.*"

Johnny obeyed. Mark told Nick to turn on the interior light for at least ten seconds, risky or not. The three of us in the back seat saw it at the same time and gasped. Johnny had a five-inch rip in the skin over his hip bone. Blood seeped slowly but steadily out. "Look at that!" Dr. Mark exclaimed. "Some of the subcutaneous fat tissue pushed out through the wound. Man, oh man." Only he would know what that word, subcutaneous, meant.

"Nick, drive us to the hospital. He's going to need stitches," I ordered. "And turn that cassette off! Now isn't the time to listen to Eddie shredding a guitar solo. We need to think …"

"Oh, shut up, Tommy! It's not even Van Halen, mister know-it-all!" Nick shouted at me from the driver's seat. Surprised by his overreaction, our eyes met in the rearview mirror and I instantly understood. Nick said, "Sorry, Tom. Didn't mean anything by it. Just stressed." I nodded that we were cool. Nick flipped off the radio, the electric wailing stopped, and all you could hear was our anxious breathing.

Johnny had taken a minute to think about my hospital demand. "No! No hospitals!" he protested. "What's the first thing they'll do? They'll call our parents! Then we'll have to come clean about how I got this. You guys want me to tell my dad, the cop, where we were? Trespassing on the grounds of Rolling Hills Country Club? Bad idea. Hey, Nicky, you want to fill in your hot-tempered father? Maybe lose the basketball scholarship you're counting

19

on for college because this'll go on your record as breaking and entering, not a silly high-school prank? Or you, Tom, you with your straitlaced parents? Most of all, how about you, Mark? I can picture it now: 'Oh hey, Dr. Mark Sr., er, Dad. Um, we're at the hospital getting our pal sewn up. Yes, he was in bad shape after getting hurt running from security *at the country club we belong to*. What did you say? No, I don't think any of the other doctors you golf with on Fridays saw us there ...' Follow me, guys? All of us will get in an insane amount of trouble." In spite of his pain, Johnny's take was spot on. None of us could mount a decent counterargument.

"Message received," I granted. "Listen, drop Johnny and me off at my house. I'll look after him until morning. We stay over at each other's houses all the time on weekends. Nothing odd about it. Besides, my parents will already be in bed. They won't know a thing."

Hearing no better suggestions, everyone agreed. We pulled up in front of my driveway. Nick hurried from the driver's seat to help Johnny out. He was slowly walking him around the car to where we waited. Dr. Mark Jr., still in healer mode, leaned in close so they wouldn't hear him say it.

"You can't fix this, Tommy. Only a real doctor can."

* * *

It was the longest night in my life, helping Johnny hold a washcloth against the gash. He wanted to roll a joint to kill the pain and carried a nickel bag and rolling papers around with him. I shut his idea down, saying not in my house. He was a solid friend and one of us, but his taste for pot was legendary. We thought it might become a problem for him down the road. Not that we were altar boys, but Nick, Mark, and I stuck mainly with beer.

With us three, we pictured our futures somewhere else. In exciting big cities, sunbaked coastal towns, or any places less degenerate than here after we graduated. Mark was too advantaged not to make something of himself, Nick too gifted athletically, and me, too keen on seeing the wider world. We didn't want our plans derailed by becoming stoners. Johnny didn't seem to share this dream. Unlike us, when he talked about life after high school, he didn't separate himself from Plainfield.

The night dragged. I gave him my bed while I lay on the floor right next to it. In our juvenile brains, Johnny and I hung onto the idea that because we were young and almost immortal, his ripped side would heal itself overnight. So, when I peeled away the blood-soaked cloth about five in the morning and we saw how much worse it looked, panic set in. The wound had swelled and the sliced skin on either side had turned almost inside out. Saturated now, droplets of blood leaked from the cloth and stained the sheets on my bed. My mother would have a righteous meltdown once she saw this. We had no choice. Mark had been right. I couldn't fix this. None of us could. Johnny needed to get to the hospital, no matter the consequences for the rest of us.

An hour after I woke up my parents, we sat numbly in the emergency room at Plainfield Memorial. They had rolled Johnny back and whether from shock or loss of blood, he blacked out. The clock on the wall showed 7:16 a.m. My mom phoned Johnny's parents, who were on their way. Fifteen minutes later, Sergeant Malone and his wife arrived. I expected to get chewed out something terrible by him and my father. Strangely, but maybe 'cause I looked like something the cat dragged in, they talked gently to me, as if I was the injured one. The sergeant surprised me by saying thank you for bringing his son here and went so far as to shake my hand. He didn't seem to be the hard-as-nails guy that Johnny painted him to be. Next, he and his Mrs. went back behind the "staff only" doors where my friend was being treated. Staring at me with worried faces, my parents asked if I needed anything. When I said no, Dad went in search of a coffee machine. Mom hurried off to find the ladies' room.

I lied. I wasn't fine. At all. I was *really* worried. About Johnny's torn side. About the dressing down that inevitably awaited me. About the moronic stunt itself. Making all of it worse was my exhaustion. I hadn't slept for a day and a half. My stomach rumbled with hunger after not eating for eighteen hours too. A sour taste filled my mouth, and I knew that even if I could somehow get some food at this unholy hour, I'd probably just throw up. In the same spot as Johnny's rip, my own side started killing me. My head seemed light as a balloon. The room was tilting to one side. I was slipping away from myself ... to where?

Nurses, doctors, and other staff came and went through the lobby. One stopped to ask if I was ready to go back and get evaluated, but I said no because I didn't want my parents to wonder where I went. Then came other passersby. They were so loud it hurt. Not in words, though. Mentally. A nurse who didn't appear much older than me rushing by railed ... *why am I always working on weekends? I'm so sick of the graveyard shift on Saturday mornings! Shift supervisor Gelfman always schedules me for the weekends. Why not the other nurses? Because I'm the newest hire and they have seniority is how she always explains it. She's such a witch ...* Catching this on the airwaves struck me as strange. The last thing I cared about was overhearing anyone else's problems. I was too out of sorts myself. It didn't stop with this nurse. Others piled on.

Most of what came to me was trivial. Some of it wasn't. Two

medical technicians wheeled in an older lady on a gurney wearing an oxygen mask. As they handed off their patient, the bald one was betting ... *that old bird ain't gonna make it. 'Course we didn't exactly rush over to her house when the dispatcher called us. Had to finish my coffee and donut. Oh well, she's lived long enough. Gotta die sometime* ... While the other attendant busied himself with ... *clocking out in forty-four minutes ... then eggs and bacon, biscuits and gravy. Can't wait to follow that with tailgating at the stadium before the Reds game. Remember to call my brother to remind him it's his turn to fill up the cooler* ... He showed no concern for whether his patient lived or died.

A few minutes later, the doctor who first met us in the lobby before taking Johnny back sauntered out from the secure treatment area. We made brief eye contact but he didn't stop to update me. With Mom and Dad away, he could drop the compassionate doctor act. As he passed, he was thinking ... *idiotic teenagers. They don't have the sense God gave a billy goat at that age. The one with the suppurated laceration might have gotten sepsis. If he had, it could've meant an infection, ICU, and in a worst-case scenario—death. That one sitting there looking at me waited seven hours to bring in his friend? Was I that clueless when I was young?* He smiled at no one in particular while this sarcastic monologue played in his head.

Somehow it got worse. Ignoring the ailing people scattered around the lobby, two new doctors with surgical masks draped around their necks strolled casually in and out of the ER. It seemed they were coming out of an operation because the other staff parted like the Red Sea when these two gods appeared. Only they weren't thinking like gods. There was nothing noble or pure or higher in their thoughts. *He's a married man, but he is so into me. I like him too. Guess I should never say never. As chief of surgery, he could help me in my career* ... the female considered. The male had his own ideas about her. Sexual things. Things at sixteen that I didn't know a married person would consider doing with someone he wasn't married to. Yuck.

All the mental chatter made me feel even sicker than I was. I'd have given anything to run away from this room. For a place of healing, the vibes here seemed so twisted. When I felt myself hit rock bottom, I said in a whisper, "Help me, God. I'm not up for this. Make it stop. I don't want to hear any more. I just wanna think about Johnny and him getting fixed up."

Right then, on the far side of the lobby, a shrieking started. A swarm of people in white ran to a kid convulsing in pain. This hospital must be the Tenth Circle of Hell. We recently read Dante's *The Inferno* in lit class and I couldn't not compare its torments to the emotional ones present in this place. Miraculously, a couple minutes later the screaming stopped as abruptly as it started. It had gotten quiet inside of my head too. My prayer must have been granted.

Mom came back from the restroom and asked what the ruckus had been. Her words put a bookend on the eavesdropping I didn't want or ask for. Sometimes, it started like it did today—when a person around me was hurting. Here there were plenty of those. Still, what made today bizarre was how long it lasted. And how I could actually feel in myself what other people were feeling. Until now, these episodes might go on for twenty seconds. This one lasted a full five minutes. It was totally disorienting. Another difference this morning was that I usually "heard" people when I was sharp and in focus. Neither of those things were true this time. Of course, nothing about the last twenty hours made sense to me. Clear your mind and stop thinking, period, I told myself. Closing my eyes, my mind wandered until I fell asleep sitting in one of those miserable hospital chairs.

Dad woke me up. He had just returned from speaking with Sergeant Malone. My friend would be fine after getting a dozen stitches and an antibiotic shot. Johnny would be released in a little while.

What I knew was coming occurred after we got home. My father asked me to sit down with him and demanded the whole story. He grounded me for a month after a marathon question-and-answer session that ended with how I better decide what kind of person I wanted to be: upstanding or a punk. He also warned me away from booze, informing me that his branch of the Connor clan struggled with the bottle. He didn't want me falling into the same hole. Until this talk, I never knew why he didn't touch the stuff when his relatives got hammered at family outings. It was a family legacy he was determined to avoid.

Worn out and muddled, my lame defense was that I was an A-student, lettering in track, and helped deliver food baskets to hungry families before each holiday with his St. Vincent DePaul group. He was in no mood for my wonder-boy commercial. Who could blame him? A month it would stay.

* * *

In my circle of friends, Haves and Could Haves, most of us were either smarter or luckier. Mark, born with all the advantages, graduated from an elite university and followed up with an MBA from Wharton. He became a partner in an investment banking firm on Wall Street.

A star basketball player, Nick's prospects dimmed after a knee injury his freshman year at a Big Ten school. With his ticket to glory gone, he lost interest in college and eventually dropped out. Disillusioned by a series of dead-end jobs, he opted to start fresh, found his way to coastal Georgia, and launched a plumbing company of his own. Between a thriving business, happy marriage, and three daughters, his life turned out fine.

Only Johnny didn't make it. He couldn't resist the siren song of a town that ensnared so many. Becoming a cop himself, he later got busted along with a dozen others in blue. Their crime: taking bribes from a drug distribution ring to look the other way. Last we heard, he got booted off the force and shunned by his family. A few years later, no one could say where he was or what happened to him.

Plainfield endured. For another couple of decades, Dynotec fouled the air and tainted the river. Its golden age ended in the early 2000s. The heady days of jobs aplenty and residents awash in cash dried up when the company's owners outsourced their manufacturing to union-free, cheaper factories in Asia. With the curtain finally descending on an era that townies thought would never end, the substance abuse ratcheted up. Only now it was driven by desperation. If the plant closing hurt the regional economy, it crushed the hedonistic way of life. Plainfield, the way it once partied, lived only in memories. Those who experienced it did not mourn its passing. A new town, one of possibilities rather than self-destruction, might rise from its human ruins someday.

As for me and my family, turned out that we were just passing through. Dad got bored with his job like he always did and moved on to a better one. Mom went with him. We stayed long enough for my sisters and me to graduate from Plainfield High. As for me, I spent the rest of my time there with my nose in the books or training at the track, reduced my social calendar, and tried hard not to disappoint my parents' lofty expectations again. Then came college, which one to attend, what to study, and those other pressing questions central to young adulthood you get to decide only once. When I eventually took this next step, I relocated to another city. Although it lay less than thirty miles away, it was a welcome return to normal.

Of course, you can't see what's waiting around the next bend in the road. It's the best and the worst thing about life. In my case, it would be both.

CHAPTER 3
FAMILIES

Living on my own, the ink still drying on my doctoral diploma, I took a job as an assistant professor of psychology at a prestigious university. We had a highly regarded medical school, law school, intercollegiate athletics program, and more than thirty thousand students. It was a promising start for someone of twenty-six and implied years of stimulating work.

When the time for graduate school arrived, I couldn't have been readier. As the sole son of a prosperous man, I bucked my father's expectations—law school—to pursue a career in higher education. It wasn't the relaxed schedule of professors, interaction with intelligent people, or even teaching which drew me to this field. It was *learning* that I couldn't resist. To spend a lifetime studying the world's great minds, ideas, and books, yet only scratch the surface of Knowledge, was too tantalizing for me to pass up.

However, with my schooling complete and now gainfully employed, calls to settle down increased dramatically from those initiated into this blissful state. For young midwesterners, the script was all too familiar. Follow it without question, conventional wisdom decreed. Families and the ties between them formed the bedrock of regional culture. Ohio might be a peculiar quilt work of rolling green meadows and gritty cities, expansive farms and massive factories, Amish enclaves and multigenerational farms in some parts offset by innovation centers and urban hipsters in others, but family life remained the stitching holding it together. Marriage and having children preserved this holy order.

While I couldn't deny a certain appeal existed to this imagery, it was too soon for me. Not having seen much of the world, and having been too busy with my education to find romance, such a traditional view struck me as unbearably dull. A good job, pretty wife, a McMansion in the suburbs, then children, neatly depicted what my next thirty years would look like. Is that all there was? Should I be content with this? Frustrated I couldn't come up with an alternative, I resigned myself to this disappointing destiny. Predictability rather than adventure, it seemed, would rule my future.

Fortunately, the Almighty must have been listening in to my musings and decided to intervene. He was aware of something even my closest friends were not: I was lonely. To this point, education had been the all-consuming focus of my life. As much as it exercised my mind, it did nothing to stir my heart. Theories, facts, or formulas couldn't compare to my secret wish for a genuine romance.

Naturally, I was kept in the dark until this greater plan began to unfold. The starring figure in it entered the scene one day and threw my orderly existence into perfect chaos. In a way, my life actually started the moment we met. Well, *collided*, really.

* * *

Bam. I took the full force of the impact on my left side, just inside the building's main entrance. It stopped me in my tracks, but since I was larger, she absorbed the worst of it. Staggering back to recover her balance, all I first saw was the top of her long-maned head. She bounced against the receptionist's desk, but its sturdiness prevented her from falling to the ground. Behind the desk, Kathy, our motherly receptionist, extended a hand to steady the poor girl. Although Kathy and I had been reviewing my appointment calendar minutes before, and I was the one rammed, chivalry demanded the high road be taken.

"Oh no! Let me help you. Are you okay? I'm so sorry." Apologies streamed from my mouth. Composing herself, the girl shook her head yes, then straightened up to her full height. I took in a view of her lovely profile when she thanked Kathy for lending a hand. Then she tuned to face me.

"How embarrassing. I've walked through that door a dozen times and never done anything like th …" She stopped speaking the minute our eyes met. Instantly, they locked. I tumbled into hers headlong. All ambient sound and movement stopped. The office setting around us melted away. Silly grins creased our faces. Frozen in this moment, we just stood there staring at each other, wide-eyed. For how long, I couldn't say.

"OH MY!" From miles away, Kathy's voice broke into our idyll. Peripherally, I saw her head swiveling from me to the girl, from the girl back to me. Kathy witnessed and testified to a love-at-first-sight moment. Perceptive woman. She was right on the mark.

"Uhhh, hi! I'm Tom. Tom Connor. And *you* are?" The girl's café au lait eyes were bottomless pools. I couldn't tear myself away from them.

"Talk about an awkward way to meet ... yeesh. Oh hey, I mean hi! I'm Alli. Pleasure to meet you after that bumpy introduction." We both laughed and shook hands. Neither hurried to let go.

"Is that short for Allison, then?"

"Actually, no. Alessa. Don't say it. I know it's different. Then again, so are my parents. My dad was born in Italy, my mother in Virginia." She smiled again, perhaps at the thought of their unlikely union.

"Works for me," I replied happily. Mesmerized, it was hard to get out a coherent sentence. We stood there staring at each other in front of the reception desk until Kathy recommended we move away from the entranceway before someone else ran into us. "I think you two need to go and chat," she added coyly. After observing the lightning strike, she was giving us our first piece of romantic advice. "Take your time, too," she winked at me.

Alli and I moved to the other side of the lobby where there was a coffee bar and snacks for students visiting the campus advising center. Luckily, no one else happened to be in the waiting room. "Want a cup of coffee?" Wow. What a brilliant opening. I felt too giddy to manage anything more sophisticated.

"Nah, I'm not much of a coffee drinker. Besides, I gotta get going. I'm already late for my next delivery." She crinkled the bridge of her nose while speaking. I took this nonverbal cue to hint she wouldn't mind lingering a little longer.

"Oh, do you work on campus too? I teach as well as do some advising here."

"Yep. For the time being I work here." A chorus of hallelujahs rained down from above, though no one heard them but me. She continued, "Majored in journalism but haven't found a position suited to my talents. I settled for a summer job writing copy for university communications until I land my first real gig out there in the wider world. At this moment, it's super exciting stuff like these brochures on why students should meet with their advisors. Like you." She tilted her head toward me and smiled wide. Her confidence in what was unfolding between us was contagious. I gladly caught it too.

"Then you've come here before to drop things off? How did I ever miss you?"

"Probably 'cause you … were … in … an … appointment … telling a student which classes to take." She dragged out the words to accent what I must have been doing to have missed her. The teasing proved to be another good sign. Beauty, boldness, and a sense of humor. I fell harder by the second.

"Well, I better get going. More publications to deliver in the back of the golf cart they give me."

"Must you leave so soon?" My heart skipped a beat at the thought of her leaving.

"I have quite a few more boxes to drop off, so I probably should. My boss isn't the understanding type." Then those eyes twinkled. She tilted her head toward me, as if to tell a secret. "But … I could come back sometime. Even later today after I'm done with my last delivery. Think you'll still be here?" Beethoven's *Ode to Joy* roared in the background but like before, no one noticed except for me.

"Of course! What time will that be?" I blurted out more desperately than I wanted to sound.

She didn't respond to my question but instead shifted topics. "Hey, are those sunglasses in your top pocket?"

"Yes. Why?"

"It's August. Midafternoon. Sweltering. Blindingly bright. You get to stay here while I venture back into that blast furnace. Let me borrow your shades, if you have no objection. Need them more than you." With that, she poached them from my pocket and marched toward the doorway.

"Hey! Wait! How will I get them back? I don't even know your last name. It's a big university."

"I guess you'll just have to find me. You're smart enough, aren't you?" With an impish smile, she bounced out the door.

Three months later to the day, we were engaged. Life rarely unfolds the way you imagine. In ways you don't foresee, it often turns out better.

* * *

My mother told me that you don't just marry the girl you love but her family too, so you better get along with them before tying the knot. Hers was sage advice.

If Alli was a wonder to me, her family was a revelation. They abounded with traits that mine did not. Animated, spontaneous, fun-loving, she and her two sisters squeezed the most out of every day. I soon saw that they inherited this zest for living from their father, Gianni. Publicly, he Americanized his name to John, but at home he would always be their Gianni. He emigrated to the United States from Italy in his twenties. On arrival, he worked for *paisano* already here and running their own restaurants or shops. Given his drive and herculean work ethic, Gianni saved enough to attain his dream and open his own place. *Capri,* named in honor of his island birthplace, was a modest, prosperous, but most decidedly, a family affair. Alli, the eldest, Mia in the middle, and Katia the baby, all worked there in assorted roles: waitressing, cooking, bussing tables, dishwashing, from junior high school through college. Their lives were a beehive of activity.

As is customary with family-owned eateries, I found, it was

habit after exhausting days of serving others, that they reserved some of the best food, wine, and conversation for themselves after closing. Close friends sometimes attended, and on occasion, even the boyfriends got invited. These socials were never dull once the wine started flowing and the highs and lows of their workday were brought up, talked over, and wisely forgotten. Tomorrow would start as a clean slate, a healthy approach that allowed them to keep up the grind day after day. Alli's mother, Nora, ran the home front as astutely as her husband operated the café. She didn't drink or carry on like the others, but every now and then came to these gatherings to keep them from too much revelry. *Capri* opened at 8 a.m. sharp each day, whether or not their heads pounded from too much chianti the night before. Together, they formed an intricate mosaic, each one sparkling in his or her own right, yet even more beautiful when taken as a whole.

For me, it was fascinating to see how much joy they derived from one another's company. Alli attributed it to their Mediterranean blood. She explained: we talk constantly, argue frequently, make up quickly, and love fiercely. It didn't take long to see this for myself. The first time that I met the Ranna family, I heard more declarations of parental and sibling love than I'd heard over the last five years. They were uninhibited about demonstrating it too. I discovered this for myself in the rash of shoulder rubs, hugs, double cheek kisses, and toasts showered on me during my welcome-to-the-Italian-community gala after we announced our engagement. In spite of the public affection, my acceptance into the fold wasn't a foregone conclusion. Unknowingly, I had offended the patriarch and he wasn't about to forget my slight without a challenge.

During the festivities, in the wake of multiple anisettes, Gianni pulled me aside. Although surrounded by others, he read me the riot act for not seeking his permission before I popped The Big Question. To him, this was an unforgiveable breach of etiquette.

"In my village on Capri, no boy would think of proposing to a man's daughter without first getting the blessing of her father. But in America, anything goes. Well, not with me!" No doubt that people in our vicinity heard him rebuke me. Regardless, his face didn't show a trace of embarrassment and those black irises bored a hole through me. This was a matter of honor. It didn't seem prudent to remind him I wasn't a boy but a man of twenty-seven. Also, even though he was much smaller than me, I was a little afraid of him.

Admitting my ignorance of Old World custom, followed by profuse apologizing—which he let me continue doing until enough fellow revelers heard my groveling—we were able to patch things up. He seemed to appreciate the willingness to humiliate myself as a sign of how much I loved Alli. Not to mention, showing deference to him. His mood suddenly softened. "It's okay. Maybe you did not understand this before. You may ask my permission *now*." He was serious despite dozens of other people standing by and listening.

Life boils down to a few pivotal moments. Aware that this was one of mine, I rose to the challenge. Alli was worth it.

"Gianni, I am madly in love with your daughter. I promise that whatever comes our way, she'll get the best part of it. I'll always take care of her in a way that would make you proud. I swear she'll never want for anything. I'm sorry I didn't ask you earlier. May I have your blessing, and *permission*, to marry her?" As if on cue, the noise level in the room plummeted, hinting that he wanted this climax to happen within view and voice range of his friends. Maybe it was my imagination, but I felt certain a number of heads inclined toward us, waiting for his reaction. Alli and Nora, whom I spied through the crowd, watched warily from the kitchen. Gianni cleared his throat and spoke.

"Yes, I grant it. All is forgiven. Now you can be my son-in-law!" His smoldering eyes twinkled. The crowd exhaled with relief, and Alli and Nora beamed at me. With gusto, he clapped me on the back and we sealed our mutual good will with an anisette that his best friend, Piero, handed to us.

* * *

My own upbringing seemed dull by comparison. We Connors lived more in our heads than hearts and spent a lot of time pursuing our own interests. Growing up, supper was the established hour where we collected after school or work. Generally, we ate and discussed and politely parted. When the meal ended, we retreated back into our own friends, hobbies, books, or television programs.

When it came to displays of affection, my family reserved them for special events such as birthdays or the holidays. Even then, it was dispensed in small quantities and solely by the women—Mom, grandmothers, and a handful of aunts. My memories didn't include a single instance of a sober male relative showing emotion of the softer kind. To his credit, my father broke with Connor stoicism periodically. Still, it was difficult to stray too far from behaviors that prior generations ingrained in him. Regardless of the male relatives' aloofness, however, there was never any doubt my parents, sisters, and I loved one another. The main difference was that among the Connors, it manifested itself in small deeds rather than oversized words.

With the Rannas, no one labored for affection. Like a natural spring, it just flowed out from each of them onto the others. Alli was particularly close to her sisters. Katia, as the baby, they fawned over most. No matter how much attention they heaped on her, she craved more. Her opposite was Mia, the middle child, who marched to her own beat. Independent and confident, she didn't run everything by Nora or Gianni before doing what she wanted. Mia trusted her own judgment and expected family members to give her the freedom to be her own person. They simply let her.

Alli adored them all. Soon, I did too. I saw how each contributed something unique to the layers of my wife's personality. There was both a style and a substance to the Rannas, my future family, which enchanted me. I had to be the luckiest man on earth to be part of two families whose stark differences somehow melded together to make an ideal world for Alli and me to begin our journey.

* * *

Twelve months after destiny brought us together, we married. With sizable student loans to repay and Alli still not working full-time in journalism, times were tight. To make meager ends meet, we rented a cramped apartment in a tired section of the city. It was all we could afford. The location scared off more than a few of our friends and relatives nestled out in statelier suburbs. We understood their hesitation. The shrill whining of police sirens fractured the late-night air at least once a week. Yet back then, nothing bad could touch us. With visitors scarce, it gave us time to delve deeper into each other. We were poor as church mice, but wildly happy.

On our first anniversary, Alli envisioned a special dinner. She scoured cookbooks, consulted with her mother, even checked for ideas with Gianni at his café, to land upon the perfect choice.

Once settled—a secret she wanted to "surprise" me with—she set about her task methodically. She tracked down and went to buy healthy ingredients at an organic food store, which were hard to find in those days. She visited home and raided her father's garden for fresh herbs to provide the proper flavors. When the much-anticipated day arrived, she prepared everything as meticulously as a trained chef. Calling her minute preparations a labor of love would be an understatement. A final preliminary: telephone my office to remind me to be home in precisely two hours when her creation came out of the oven. During this time, Alli set an elegant table, including a hand-embroidered table linen that we received as a wedding present from her relatives in Calabria. She had been saving it for this milestone anniversary.

Playing my part, I left work promptly on my own mission. Knowing that payday wasn't for another week, I hoarded my last twenty dollars to buy the best bottle of supermarket champagne. I felt just as excited about our special celebration as she did.

Minutes after arriving home to delicious smells coming from the kitchen, I filled two crystal flutes that we also received as a gift. The excitement peaked as Alli tiptoed in from the kitchen carrying her prize creation—a magnificent *Caprese* casserole. She was holding the bowl by its ceramic arms. Three steps from the table, one of the arms snapped off. The bowl, casserole inside, and her hopes shattered to pieces on the floor. Stunned at first, Alli turned to me, doe-eyed. Then she started to cry.

"It's okay, honey. Really it is." I hurried to hug her. "Don't worry. It's the thought and effort that counts. Let's just clean it up, then go out and splurge instead."

Wiping away tears, Alli sniffled, "*With what?* All the money we had left went into the casserole. Now it's splattered all over the tile. There's nothing left to 'splurge' with. We're broke. There's

38

no money left at all!"

"Hmm. Not sure that's true," I countered, after having a brainstorm on how to salvage the evening. "Gimme a few minutes."

I ran out to my car and searched the middle console. A couple bucks and some scattered change was there. Next, I went to her jalopy and scrounged only a handful of quarters. Back inside, I checked the kitchen drawers but came up empty. There was one last place to go. I jammed my hand between and under the couch cushions. Eureka—a five was wedged in there! All told, we cobbled together $7.36.

"See?! We *can* go out!" Buoyed by this princely sum, we drove to Taco Bell, ordered as many tacos as our riches allowed, and feasted like royalty in the front seat of my car. In between bites, we laughed and poked and teased each other like kids. There would never be another anniversary we remembered more fondly than this first one.

Time was on our side. We were young and optimistic. Our future teemed with possibilities. Opportunity soon came knocking at work. I shifted into an administrative role at the university paying significantly more and acquired my first title: Assistant Dean. By sheer determination and refusing to take no for an answer, Alli landed a coveted job at a local magazine. She spent a couple of years learning the publishing business from the inside. Then she parted ways to start her own communications firm. She kept it manageable—just her and two other employees—aware that children were likely at some stage in the near future.

Absorbed in the pleasant rhythms of this life together, things hummed smoothly along. Everything was beautiful. Until a telephone call destroyed it one crisp September morning.

* * *

Stepping along the hallway to my office, I heard the telephone ringing. It stopped, then immediately started all over. Not a good sign. What now? Another flash mob student protest about climate change at the provost's office? A demonstration and counterprotest between Young Democrats and Young Republicans that devolved into conflict? Or, the call I dreaded, a suicide in one of our residence halls. Those were the worst because it fell to me to take on the miserable task of notifying the parents. I shuddered, fighting a sense of foreboding, and betting it must be this last prospect.

I hustled to my desk and grabbed the phone. Kathy, who accompanied me after the promotion, came on the line. There was an urgent call from my wife. Unfortunately, she couldn't make out what Alli was trying to say. She was sobbing too hard to understand. Something has the poor dear beside herself, Kathy noted uneasily.

Adrenalin pumped into my veins and as my heart pounded, I released the hold button. Alli? What's wrong? Between gasps, she told me that Mia was hurt. She had been in a terrible car accident. It was bad. Very bad. An ambulance rushed her to the emergency room. The police would say nothing more. We needed to get to the hospital as soon as possible. Alli was at her parents' house. Nora and Gianni had already left. Sit tight, I said. Be there as soon as possible.

On the frantic drive, a flood of random thoughts surged across my mind. None of them was hopeful and I got angry at myself for presuming disaster. This could not be happening. Mia was twenty-four years old. A newlywed. With her own husband, children ahead, and the whole of life in front of her. In the car, I asked God to make the early reports wrong. They must be. Mia was irrepressible. Nothing could stop her. It couldn't be as bad as what we first heard.

When I reached the Rannas' house where Alli waited, these fears materialized. Tears streaming down her face, she collapsed into my arms. *Mia was gone.* Nora telephoned from the hospital to tell her.

CHAPTER 4
THE SWEETEST THING

The funeral and grimness surrounding it crushed us. The only thing we experienced was desolation. Fortunately, I could escape the sadness by going back to work. But while away, I worried constantly about Alli and her state of mind. She refused to leave the house or call back friends who tried to check in with her through voicemails. The only breaks in her solitude came when she went to her parents' home. And they and Katia lived in the same shadows.

So, a month after our tragedy, I convinced the woman I loved to go out on a date with me. Reconnecting with life as it pulsed around us would do her a world of good. Too many days I watched her suffering from across a great divide. Alli had separated herself from the rest of humanity to cope with the grief. I felt the pain of this loss too, but not as intensely. Mia was *her* sister. They were as close as two siblings could be. Wanting to do right as her husband, my goal this evening was to throw a lifeline over this divide and pull Alli back, even temporarily, to the way things used to be.

I suggested *The Dubliner*. It was an upscale bistro posing

as an Irish-themed tavern that we often frequented. When they weren't playing Celtic folk songs, the paneled walls reverberated with Van Morrison, Thin Lizzy, The Chieftains. For us, it was a place of fond memories and familiar faces: college friends, excellent pub fare, imported ales, and where, less than a month after our predestined meeting, Alli and I could take the suspense no longer and madly declared our love for each other. Tonight, four years later, those happy memories lay buried under a mountain of despair. She suffered so much that apart from her parents' house, she hadn't gone anywhere, including her own office. Public places carried too much risk. Her fear was that despair might suddenly overwhelm her, a flood of tears would fall, and she'd make a spectacle of herself before prying eyes. Which is why tonight, her consenting to my idea came as a surprise.

Although the tavern was busy for midweek, we didn't have to wait long. At my request, we were ushered to a booth in a quieter corner. Minutes later, the waiter, Ian, according to his name badge, graced our table. We got off on the wrong foot immediately. I disappointed him by ordering iced tea.

You could tell instantly that a customer not ordering alcohol—a crucial variable in the final tip amount—troubled him. "Are you sure? We have eight imported ales on tap and twelve others available in bottles. Though it ended forty minutes ago, I'll still give you happy-hour pricing ..." he bartered.

"Thank you, but no," I said. "It's a weekday. I'll stick with iced tea."

"Ma'am? You?" He turned toward Alli, hoping maybe she might be swayed. He leaned on one foot while shaking the other one nervously. Too many energy drinks before he started his shift, it seemed.

"Nothing for me. Oh ... I'm sorry. To drink? Iced tea too, I guess." Alli's voice came from far away. So much for achieving his objective.

"Any appetizers at least, then?"

"We haven't gotten that far yet. Maybe by the time you return with our drink order," I politely offered.

"Mmm ..." He checked himself before the eye roll went too far to conceal. The waiter slid his pad and pen back in his apron pocket without writing anything down and left.

"What looks good tonight, Alli?" I asked, a trifle too cheerfully. Her eyes roamed vacantly over the menu. Trying to make conversation, I ran through some options we might consider, attempting to make each sound more delicious than it was. Projecting positivity might improve her mood.

"Don't know, yet. Maybe the shepherd's pie. It says the owner makes it just like his mother did back in County Sligo," she said spiritlessly.

"Sligo. That's a province in northwestern Ireland. My father traced a branch of his family back there ..." I volunteered, aiming to ignite a wider conversation. About Ireland, traveling there, ancestry, anything, but it fell flat so I let my voice trail off. Although familiar to us from past patronage, Alli kept her eyes on the menu like she was seeing it for the first time.

Ian the waiter returned with our drinks, a basket of rolls, and took our dinner order. I went with the corn beef and cabbage in an effort to tap the lively spirit of the tavern. While Alli ordered, he looked around and stopped only when his gaze landed at the main entrance. His attention was clearly there.

"Excuse me. Did you get down what I ordered?" my wife gently asked.

"Uh, yes. I did. The shepherd's pie with a small dinner salad," he repeated, still alternating his glance between us and the foyer.

After vindicating himself by correctly restating her order, he scurried away. The level of background noise around me picked up a notch. Only it wasn't coming from the other patrons in the bar. It was inside my head.

"Charming guy. Wonder what's up with him?" Alli said matter-of-factly, not really expecting an answer.

"He's worried about his girlfriend. They had a wicked fight and now he's afraid she's serious about ending it." Words spilled out without even thinking about her question, from a mysterious yet indisputable source.

Alli put on a puzzled expression. "Nice guesswork, Tom. How'd you come up with that? Although, I'll grant what you just made up is as possible as anything."

I didn't tell her it wasn't made up. Flashes of what happened before this server came to work scrolled across my mind. Piecing them into a mental movie, I saw him and a girl having an argument, her saying it was over and that she'd drop by the restaurant later to give him back his keys after she moved out her things. She told him that she wasn't ever coming back and proved it with a stinging slap across his face. Terrified she meant it this time, his distant demeanor made sense.

Still, I wanted no part of his melodrama. Already, my own cheek started smarting in the same place his took the hit. My concentration had to remain fixed on creating a pleasant outing for Alli. To reacquaint her with the lighter side of life, my sole ambition. I shut down the last flickering images of Ian and the raging girlfriend on my inner movie screen.

We were alone again, in the amber glow of electric candlelight from a sconce on the wall. I fought the good fight by raising assorted topics, striving to keep Alli in the moment. I talked about whatever I could so as not to surrender to the silence. She perceived this and her feeble laughs at my sillier remarks showed an appreciation for the efforts. Only she couldn't find her voice. The sorrow weighing down on her had stolen even that.

"I wonder what's taking so long? The service here gets worse every time we come. It's nothing like the old days." My desperation gave ground to irritability. If I couldn't provide the relief she deserved by distracting her with an enjoyable dinner date, someone else would feel my wrath. "I hadn't really noticed." Alli dithered with her silverware.

As if to prove how foolish my comments were, the waiter returned moments later, slid our entrees before us and bolted. Good. The food gave us a reprieve. Silence hung over the table while we ate. Internally, I racked my brain for a fresh, interesting topic. Then, I had a stroke of genius.

"Hey, what will you want for dessert?" A more loaded question there could not be. If my wife had a weakness, it was her sweet tooth. All the Ranna women suffered from it, but Alli was afflicted the worst. Friends teased her about poring over dessert options on any menu before choosing her main course, a sin to which she gladly confessed. Especially any treat heavy on chocolate. Unfortunately, my brilliant idea fell apart as fast as it arose. In a sign of how out of sorts she felt, Alli waved off my question with a sweep of her hand. That did me in. The well inside was dry.

A rowdy group, beer bottles in hand and playfully cussing each other, passed by on their way to a party room in the back. One of them, the last in line, peeled off and stopped at our booth. Hold on. She wasn't part of this bunch. Turned out she was one of the managers. Well, a manager is what I assumed her to be. She didn't have on the standard server's white button-down shirt and black trousers. Instead, she wore a blue satin blouse and a navy skirt. Covered plate in hand, she greeted us.

"Hello! How was your dinner tonight? Fine, I hope." She studied us while waiting for our answer.

"Everything was good," I answered. There seemed to be something familiar about her. Alli teased that I said this a lot about people I had just met. But she was wrong. My applying it to any stranger was a rarity.

The manager smiled wide, happy to receive my compliment on the food. To be inclusive, she also sought validation from Alli. "Ma'am? How was it for you?"

"Oh … Good. Very good, actually," my wife said, a tad embarrassed she hadn't issued any praise before being prompted.

The staffer nodded in gratitude, then set the covered plate in front of us. Grinning at our anticipation of its contents, she took her time lifting the lid. Before us was a mound of ice cream melting on a double-sized brownie, caramel oozing down the sides. A massive slice of Snickers Pie sprawled decadently across the platter.

Delicious as it looked, I didn't understand. "It looks wonderful but this must be a mistake. We didn't order this." In truth, we hadn't seen our waiter for the last fifteen minutes. I pointed to our empty tea glasses as proof of how badly we'd been neglected.

"Oh dear. I'm sorry about that. Ian isn't having his best night. I'll chat with him." A cheerful sort, she redirected our attention back to the plate. "About this dessert … We, the management, take it upon ourselves to give complimentary desserts to valued customers. Like you two. It's a simple way to show our gratitude for your business. You two happen to be the deserving guests tonight. Hopefully, it will be the perfect ending to your evening with us. Please enjoy!" She bowed slightly, took two steps back, and soon disappeared from view after rounding a bank of high-backed booths.

I was still stuck on this unusual turn of events when Alli picked up her fork and made a move toward the pie. She checked herself. She glanced at me, then at the dish, then back at me. Water pooled in the bottom of her eyes. Unsure of the cause, I held out my napkin but she pushed it back.

"No, I don't need that. I'm still sad, but even more so, shocked." Seeing my confusion, she explained. "I was, of course, thinking about Mia the whole time you were trying to entertain me."

"Ouch. You mean to say that I'm not the dazzling conversationalist that I imagined!?" I pretended insult. Alli argued this wasn't the point.

"Don't you remember the last time you and I brought *her* here?"

Sheepishly, I admitted that I did not. "Brought *who* here, honey?"

"Let me refresh you—*Mia*. Neither she nor I cared about finishing our dinners. But as usual, both of us insisted on ending with something sweet. You were making faces at us, laughing, and saying 'of course, there go the Ranna sisters again!'" Seeing Alli brighten by memories from better times gave me a lift too.

"Don't you remember what we ordered on that occasion? It was exactly this: Snickers Pie! It was our all-time favorite dessert here. Me and Mia always shared it. Now do you see what just happened? It's Mia's way of letting me know she's close by." Color filled her cheeks and her eyes looked hopeful.

"*She's here.* I can feel her. Can't you?" Alli brimmed with optimism. Her joy, missing for so long, was contagious because in the moment, I also sensed Mia's spirit. Her personal signature in life, a crackling positive energy, filled the air in our booth. It lingered until we finished the last bite of dessert.

After savoring Mia's visit for a while and after devouring the last morsels of the treat, we were readying to leave when the waiter finally returned. Ian was confused by the traces of dessert on the plate. "How did *that* get here?" I told him it was a gift from the manager.

"The manager?" he scoffed. "What manager?"

I described the woman who delivered the sweet ending to supper.

He called me out. "Who? Rick is the manager on duty tonight," he said, aiming a finger at a salt-and-pepper-haired man barking orders to staff at the main servers' station. "I don't know who you're talking about. We don't have any female managers on duty today. What was her name, anyway?" He was determined to prove me wrong.

"Come to think of it, she didn't say. Or wear a badge with her name on it. Did she, honey?" Me stating this and Alli unable to provide much support only emboldened him.

"There is definitely no one who would wear something different from what I am wearing. It's not allowed. See for yourself. Even Rick is dressed in the same thing as me. White oxford shirt and black pants. And with a name tag! See?"

"Well, I don't know what else we can tell you. Here are the remnants of the dessert as you can plainly see. Yes, it's melted ice cream and caramel, here. Plus a few peanut fragments over there. Somebody obviously brought it to us. Neither of us went to the kitchen and took it from the freezer. All we know is that a woman wearing a blue blouse and dark skirt who carried herself like a manager put it on our table. Right, honey?" This time, Alli nobly supported me with a vigorous nod of her head before frowning at him. She resented him spoiling the mood so soon after our uplifting experience. "That's all I can tell you."

Not wanting to risk what little might be left of his tip, the waiter forced a nasty smile and left. Determined to recover the magic of a few minutes ago, I tossed some bills on the table and declared, "Let's get out of here."

Weaving our way through the crowded foyer, on the walk to the car, Alli reached for my hand. The tiniest of romantic gestures it was, but contact like this had been absent from our relationship since the accident. She was humming too. On the drive home, it felt like a load had been lifted off my shoulders. The effect on Alli was visible, hope was the third passenger in our car.

When we left home two hours ago, sorrow still overwhelmed her. Now she was squeezing my hand, singing, and smiling. Who else other than Mia could have made this happen?

The traffic light changed and I pressed down on the accelerator. We were almost home.

* * *

Lying awake in bed, I kept thinking about the scene at the tavern. Our volatile, unhappy waiter. The manager, a total enigma, who came out of nowhere and vanished back into it. The perfectly picked, perfectly timed dessert that she delivered to our table. It couldn't have been sweeter to someone so starved for hope as Alli. What an exquisite coincidence it had been.

Something my grandmother was fond of saying shook itself loose in the corners of my memory. It fitted what I had been pondering.

When we were young, my sisters and I liked listening to the conversations between our parents and grandparents. While we played with assorted toys on the family room floor, and the grown-ups sipped coffee in the kitchen, we eavesdropped. Our attachment to Grams and Gramps made it kind of a game: we waited for one of our names to come up, and if it did, we felt a surge of pride. More than a few times, we overheard Grams reminding the others that nothing important in life happened by accident. Mom might ask, oh, then you don't believe in luck? No, I don't, she declared. There's no such thing as chance in life. Coincidences are just the Lord's way of intervening without seeking credit, she'd say. For a spell afterward, none of the adults budged while they mused on her words. In the end, they must have signed on to her point of view because any further talk about the "lucky" break of cousin so-and-so or aunt such-and-such trailed off. Eventually, one of them, usually Gramps, who knew how wise Grams was, stood up, stretched his legs, and walked over to the coffee pot to refill his cup. In sequence, the rest of them would follow.

I wished my grandmother was still alive. Her advice would have been priceless on how to mend the pieces of my new family's broken hearts. My relationship with Grams had been different than everyone else. If the others didn't discern it, she and I were well aware of it. I trusted her with things no one else ever heard from me. She reciprocated. While she gave generously of herself to all of us, she gave something extra to me.

The winter of fourth grade I caught pneumonia. She came to stay at our house to help my parents. They both worked, so with them gone during the day and my sisters at school, she took charge of nursing me back to health. How many cool compresses did she put on my forehead to break a stubborn fever? How many chest massages with Vicks vapo-rub did she administer? How many times did she fluff my pillows or pull the quilt up to my chin? How many times did she wake me up to a steaming cup of tomato soup or children's aspirin tablets? Too many to count. But it was our talks that made me feel better.

On a January afternoon, with snowflakes swirling heavy outside the bedroom window, she said, "Tommy, I love your sisters to the moon and back, but you're my favorite. I never had a boy, just your mom and auntie. You're the one I missed out on." She tweaked my nose, smoothed the blanket, and told me not to tell anyone else. It would stay our secret.

While my sisters spent the day at school, she entertained me with tales from her own childhood. Her stories came from a world I could hardly imagine, *before* television, microwaves, and computers. Even radios and cars hadn't been around long when she was a little girl. She also spoke of an older sister who died from tuberculosis back in the 1940s. Remembering this made her sad, so I got sad too. But the good part of this story came when she told me her sister visited her once after she died to say she was in heaven, it was glorious, and not to cry anymore. Their meeting changed everything for Grams. From then on, she stopped fretting about Ellen. I had never heard of her sister before, not even from my own mother. But I was happy that Grams trusted me with a story this precious to her. And I didn't question it because she always and only spoke truths.

Although she died when I was in my thirties, it hit me hard. No one could replace her in my life. The homespun wisdom, the selflessness, the resilience, she was in a league of her own. No one else ever sang me to sleep when I was small and terrified of night-time thunderstorms. It was a tender mercy I never forgot. After she passed, I regretted not telling her about Lizabeth. She'd have believed my every word.

It was getting late. I rolled over onto my side. Next to me on the bed, Alli slept soundly. I prayed that she was having happier dreams instead of those frequent nightmares since Mia's accident.

She had endured enough.

One final time I traveled back to the tavern. Was it merely chance that we got chosen for the free dessert? Or Mia's coy way of sending us a message from the other side? My grandmother had a remarkable way of putting things. No need to wonder a minute more. I already knew the answer.

CHAPTER 5
RESTORATION

Grading term papers tested my stamina. It came with the territory of being a professor and I wanted to do it conscientiously. Most of my students spent hours writing these research pieces. Or at least that's what I wanted to believe.

Colleagues at the university laughed at my idealism. They reminded me that ours was the cut-and-paste internet age and to open my eyes to the cheating all around. Ignoring their cynicism, I preferred to keep the faith in my students by reading their words carefully and responding with intelligent comments. And I believed they appreciated my trust. If the number of requests I got asking me for advice on or reference letters to graduate school were an indication, my faith was justified. Students didn't ask this of teachers they didn't respect.

For better or worse, to grade well took time. A lot of it. Space, too—papers lay scattered over the floor of our den. I had been reading them for hours. An empty soda can, a handful of M&Ms, and cookie crumbs atop a crumpled napkin where I had stretched out, marked the passing of time. Outside, a thunderstorm acquiesced into a steady rain.

Inside, the clock above the fireplace showed it was a quarter to midnight. From her steady, soft breathing, I knew Alli had nodded off on the couch behind me. In front, with the sound turned down, the droning of the television acted like white noise, allowing me to get deep into my own flow. A bluish glow coming from the television merged with light spilling in from the kitchen to let me see the words on the paper surprisingly well. Working late at night or early in the morning suited me. With it quiet or asleep, the world was much more conducive to clear thinking.

Which is why a spontaneous impulse that I was being watched bewildered me. Head down and immersed in an essay, I sensed an interloper into our peaceful sanctuary. Alli hadn't budged. I surveyed our family room and ended with an unobstructed view of the kitchen. All clear.

Then the air began to buzz ever so faintly. A fuzzy patch of light coalesced by the table. Faint at first, it intensified as the seconds passed. The patch grew brighter. There appeared to be something in its center. Mesmerized, I began to see the outline of a person. He or she was brighter than the rest of the field surrounding it. I blinked hard once, twice, then roughly rubbed my eyes, straining to make plain what was forming. A face became discernible.

I could not believe what I was seeing and exclaimed, "Mia?!" No answer came. She had to finish forming. My heart raced like a sprinter's. This can't be happening. Only there she was. If her body rested in a cemetery ten miles away, her spirit shone in all its radiance no more than ten feet away.

Awed, I studied her closely. The clothing she wore looked different. Instead of her everyday jeans or skirts, she wore a gown-like garment. The gown was either made of a dazzling fabric or light itself. Although bright as the sun, it didn't hurt my eyes to look at it. The part of her body most clearly defined came from the shoulders up and seemed solid enough. From there downward, her form was less dense, with parts being translucent. Through it, I could see the kitchen countertop and open box of chocolate chip cookies we snacked on before Alli dropped off to sleep.

"Mia! Is it really you?" I questioned, although the logical, left side of my brain insisted otherwise. For a scholar firmly tethered to reality, trained in research methods, author of a textbook on statistics, seeing the soul of a deceased person was beyond the realm of reason. But it was also unlikely I had lost my grip on reality since supper time. After all, every other aspect of my life continued in its usual rhythm. And as far as I knew, the sun still rose in the east and set in the west. No, I wasn't hallucinating.

Because another part of me, more astute and reliable than the right brain, remembered that this was *exactly* how the other side operated. Everything was possible there. It was a world which operated as it pleased, in blatant yet genial disregard for the fixed rules of our reality. My warring selves and the debate between them apparently reached Mia. It tickled her. Mouth never moving, she replied accordingly.

Of course, it's me! And no, you aren't imagining this. You already had experiences with this world when you were a child. And you remember it too, don't you? This is how you know me being here isn't imaginary.

"All right. But this is still surreal. Like Lizabeth was when I was eight," which Mia knew and had referenced. "So you're like her now? Visiting us as an angel?" I used words at this point, not thought-transfer like she did.

No, no, no. I'm not an angel. I'm a person like you. She didn't speak of herself in the past tense but counted herself among the living. This choice of words reconnected her to how she had been in life. Little details mattered to her.

After considering her words, I moved on to the matter which most grieved us survivors. It was a simmering anger that refused to leave. "Why did God have to take you so young? I don't understand how he let this happen. It's so unfair!"

Mia's answer rocked me. *Unfair? Only if you put the blame on God. What if this isn't how it works? What if it was a destiny I chose myself?*

Whoa. This I did not anticipate. It's sheer opposition to how I presumed she would answer left me speechless. Talk about flipping the paradigm. What was Mia saying? That she and God worked out a shooting-star life plan, terribly short but blazingly bright? And when she achieved what she set out to do during her brief time on Earth, it was preordained to end? Such an alternative never occurred to me, to anyone who knew and loved her. It stood on its head our reasoning about why the tragedy took place. About why bad things happen to good people. About how we aren't at the mercy of fate, but in some mysterious way, play a role in determining ours.

For months afterward, Mia's words consumed a great amount of head space as I pored over its implications. *Do we somehow have a voice in the length of our lives?* However, in that moment, with her before me, it was too grand a question to settle. Already, I knew that she wouldn't be here long and didn't want to waste a second. I posed a different question.

Why did you come? To show us you survived and are in ... heaven? Switching to her mode of communication, I thought this toward her instead of speaking. It wasn't hard to get back into the groove. Lizabeth taught me how long ago.

They preferred telepathy. It provided greater clarity by removing all emotional priming in speech. For instance, if a friend said, I care so much about you, the best you could hope for was that he truly meant it. However, when one of these visitors *thought* it, you intuitively knew it came from the purest source. There was no room to misunderstand, mislead, or leave things hidden. If their thought-language wasn't as tinged with sentiment, it far outclassed our words in its effect. Later, I called how these beings communicated as *thought-said*. Amazingly, I could do it too when engaging with them. Maybe it was the first language all of us ever learned.

Mia silently shimmered while I was thinking about all this. After a deferential pause, she returned to my last question. *I'm here for Alli, not you, Tom.* If her message was blunt, her tone was benign, an example of how their truth was tempered with compassion. *The only thing I have to tell you is this: just be there for her. Be patient and kind and loving. These are what she most needs from her husband.*

That's it? Mia's advice put me off. *Of course. I can do that,* I thought-said to her. It irked me that my departed sister-in-law had come from the afterlife just to tell me to do what any decent husband would. I let Mia know it too. *Is that all? Is that the reason you're visiting? I was already doing those things for her. Or is there something else? Do you want me to wake up Alli so she can see you too? Don't you want to talk to her?*

Concentrating on Alli with a rapt expression, Mia thought-said, *Don't wake her. It's better this time if she doesn't see me. It will help with why I'm here.*

Why are you here? I pressed to solve the mystery.

On cue, Mia's luminosity surged, like a chandelier's dimmer switch turned up to its brightest setting. Her form rippled one time, then again, like waves do. Waves … ah, yes, I comprehended now. Waves of healing spiritual energy were passing from her to my wife. As she laid on the couch, Alli began to glow too, though less radiantly as she received this gift. There was a symmetry to this activity. Mia reciprocated what Alli had done so often for her when they grew up together and it was her who needed a loving, caring touch to heal from an injury. God was permitting this house call for both of them.

Realizing Mia's mission and its sisterly nature, I felt like an intruder. Better if I left them to each other. She already explained my job as husband. Now she executed hers as healer. It was all I needed to know.

I said aloud, "Thank you for coming, Mia. It means more to me than you know. That your love for her is so strong you came back to restore her. I promise to tell Alli about it. She probably won't believe me. If she wakes up feeling stronger, maybe it'll convince her I'm telling the truth."

Not wanting to interpose further, I turned and picked up where I had left off. Despite the mix of incredulity and joy, it wasn't hard to slip back into evaluation mode. The student's paper before me was making an unsupportable argument against cognitive behavioral therapy but doing it with such dash that I couldn't put it down. When I finished my assessment and gave it a "B," curiosity got the better of me. I peered at the spot where Mia last stood. A dark, empty kitchen greeted my eyes.

Tomorrow morning would arrive. It was sure to be different. Alli would wake up feeling better than she had for some time. Mia's visit would be the reason.

It was late and I was tired now. Pushing the jumble of papers away, I stretched out on the carpet. It didn't take long to fall asleep.

* * *

Confident Mia delivered on her pledge, I didn't disturb Alli until midmorning. She sounded peeved when I filled her in on the events of the prior evening.

"You what?! You *saw* her last night?! She was here?!" Alli's saucer-sized eyes engulfed mine. *"How can that be?"*

"Trust me when I say I know how deranged it sounds. But I swear that what I'm telling you is true. And, yes, she *was* here. As real as you or me, only in a different form. How she got here or where exactly she came from, I can't explain."

"You mean that you saw her like she used to be? Or as a spirit?"

"It must have ... been her soul. I can't give what I saw a definitive name. But she formed in a field of light right there in our kitchen. She looked exactly the same as the last time we saw her alive. Even more radiant. But without a doubt, it was Mia."

Disbelief dominated Alli's face, but her upset didn't stop me. "Listen, I get it. Really, I do. Communicating with her defies everything people think about reality." My choice of the *people* rather than *me* was deliberate. Given my boyhood voyage into a space outside the known real estate of the universe, my take on the frontiers of "reality" was more fluid than others.

When this door swung open for me, I was a child. Too innocent to lie about such things. Also, too young and undamaged to be delusional. My interlude with Lizabeth never felt unnatural. On the contrary, once I got past its initial strangeness—a strangeness due to what adults already instilled about how the world worked—there was something familiar, even comforting about the experience. It felt like coming *home*. All it took were a few fleeting minutes in that zone where realties mingled to recall this truth.

Which is why I chafed at the reflex in everyone else to deny or dismiss any experience which possessed even a hint of the mystical. If they seemed pure fantasy to others, they had become second nature to me. From my point of view, they were *magnificent*, absolutely. *Of a higher source*, definitely. *Inscrutable*, certainly. *Imaginary*, not a chance. Why couldn't people grant that there might be more to existence than what science decreed or our five limited senses perceived?

Alli interrupted my interior monologue, honing in on something I had said. "So you didn't just see her. You *communicated* with her too?"

"Yes," I owned up, sensitive to her doubt but getting frayed by it. Elation was what I expected from her, not cross-examination.

"Why *you*? Why in the middle of the night? And how come I didn't get to see her along with you? She was *my sister*." My wife felt cheated that she missed out on an extraordinary opportunity, one which didn't happen every day and might not again.

"You're right. She didn't come for me. She didn't come for us. *She came for you*." Hearing this from me, Alli's attitude mellowed.

"Me?"

"Uh huh."

"She came for me ..." Alli repeated. "Well ... to do what then? When I was out of it? Why would she come all the way from the afterlife to see me sleeping and not ask you to wake me up?"

"She wanted it that way."

"I don't get it. Why?"

"That I can answer because she told me straight up. It was to pour strength back into you after losing her the way we did. She knew you were suffering and in misery. Mia came to restore you."

"She actually said that was the reason why she came?"

"In so many words, yes, she did."

Alli let my statement register. Because it was important, I made the point one more time. "She came to heal you and make you stronger. She wants you to feel good again. To know that better days are ahead, and to move on with your life." I ended there. Too many words would diminish the effect of the message. Alli could weigh and decide these things for herself.

"Oh," she said, then grew silent.

Without knowing why, perhaps she did feel better this particular morning. Her stomach wasn't tied in its usual knots nor did her emotional burden seem as heavy. Today, she might avoid the trap of replaying over and over what might have been. The rain subsided. She had seen the honey blue sky peering from behind the thinning cloud cover outside. Whatever the cause, she smiled wide and said she needed to get dressed for the day ahead.

* * *

At the mercy of a broken traffic light at campus's edge, you felt their eyes on you from the ramshackle camp. This crossroads served as a terminus of the bus line from downtown. Where it ended, the homeless got dumped. Driving through it every day, I knew how they watched the cars and people driving them before deciding which ones to beg from during red lights. It creeped me out a little. My sympathy for them was strongest at a distance. Typically, I kept on moving through this intersection to make a right turn. With the signal out of commission this morning, cars going straight blocked those of us farther back in the turn lane.

During the wait, I had been spied and selected. Here he came, hobbling up to my car window which I had no choice but to lower. "Spare change, sir?" An exceptionally tall man, six and a half feet easily, he asked at the partly open window. With his hands resting on it like he might try to force it down more, I went ahead and opened it all the way. He drew uncomfortably close, his face not more than three feet from mine. A smell of dried sweat floated into the car.

"Give me a second." I rifled through my pant pockets, no simple maneuver considering the seatbelt was tight across my lap.

"Beautiful day, isn't it?" His beard was matted and clothing frayed, The Cincinnati Reds hat on his head was gray instead of its original crimson. He saw me looking at the hat and mistook it for partiality. "I'm a Reds' fan! You too?

"Mmm ... guess so." Now what should I say? "You'll need that cap. It's supposed to rain later." I hoped my remark would make him think me so dull that the grass could only be greener at the next car.

He whistled. "Nice car you have here. Dressed nice too. You work at the university?"

"I do."

"Must have a good job there." I smiled but didn't say anything back. He didn't slow down. "I had a job too, once. Was a house painter. Made a decent living at it. Then we got bought out by the bigger guys. The new foreman complained I was too slow. He kept yelling at me to hurry it up, but I wouldn't. Took pride in my work. Needed to do it the right way. My way. Not his. So they lemme go. Then one bad thing after another happened. Now here I am."

"Maybe something will open up for you soon." Not that I believed it, but at a loss on what else to offer.

"Oh, I'll be all right. I'm just thankful for another day." Tilting his head back, he let a stretching sun kiss his eyelids and took a deep breath of the cool morning air. Considering his lot, this optimism seemed oddly out of place. "What about you? Are ya thankful?"

"I'd like to think so. Although ... well ... for what exactly?" His question caught me off guard. It wasn't the kind you expected from a panhandler.

"Success, family, insights from heaven."

"Insights from heaven?" Hearing that word come out of his mouth unnerved me. Was this the real source of my experiences? Could this beggar speak with authority on this subject? Lizabeth did not say she came from heaven to save me. Nor did Mia, on her mission to heal Alli. Granted, it was certainly implicit. After all, where else could they come from? Yet although they emanated goodness, love, and an energy unlike any others, neither actually claimed a heavenly mantle. Now, their home had been revealed by a poor panhandler.

"You've been given a gift, seeing what you have. Treasure it. Along with what is still in store ... Later on, tell people what happened and what you know. Many are adrift. And alone. You can deliver hope to them." His slang disappeared. A striking elegance overtook his speech. It was no longer the banter of a beggar but the eloquence of a philosopher.

My lifelong aversion to disclosing anything of my esoteric encounters reared its stubborn head. "What if I refuse to?"

"You'll discern the importance of it and change your mind."

"*No*. I've learned it's easier not to speak of such things. People aren't ready to hear them. Or they don't want to. It shakes them up—what they think they know about life, what comes after, the structure of the universe. They end up furious that I dared disrupt the rhythms of their orderly lives and take it out on me."

Undaunted, he replied, "You'll set aside these fears ... because what you've been shown is greater than you. It must be told."

The writing was on the wall and I knew I'd already lost this battle with powers far greater than me. But in a final act of defiance, "I wouldn't count on it."

"A holder of vital knowledge who doesn't want to share it but must ..." His eyes left me and went far away for a few seconds before he wistfully added, "Like ... Jonah." As if he and the biblical figure were old friends and this was a topic of frequent debate between them. "The problem is that this knowledge isn't yours to keep."

"I am *not* remotely like Jonah," as if I had any clue what this reluctant prophet was like. All I knew was that while running from a divine summons, he got swallowed by a whale, was disgorged unhurt, and finally relented to preach as originally tasked. I was a run-of-the-mill Ohio college professor alive during an epoch in history notable for nothing. I wasn't even religious in a scripture-quoting, churchgoing sense. But this was beside the point. The Tall Man–Reds' fan couldn't force me to break my silence. Let him insist all he wanted. Because he had nothing and therefore nothing to lose. For me, too much was at stake. If I did as he instructed, there could be real and damaging consequences to my livelihood.

"Believe me, you *will* tell of it. When the time comes," he reiterated.

"All right, fine!" Worn down, I rushed to end our encounter. These messengers didn't yield an inch concerning what they came to tell you. Arguing further would be futile.

"So then, exactly how will I know when 'the time comes'?"

"You'll have an awakening, and after some hardships and soul-searching, know that the time has arrived. You'll also find the courage to tell it truthfully and without fear."

"I see." But I really didn't.

Done with fumbling for change, I remembered a ten-dollar bill for lunch Alli tucked into my shirt pocket before I left home. A few seconds later, I thrust it toward him.

"Hey, man, thanks! Have a good 'un!" Just like that, his words returned to their street style. He tottered back to the others watching us from the tent camp. Once there, he handed the ten to the sorriest-looking man in the group.

The Reds' fan, not hard to spot among the pack given his towering height and grimy baseball cap, wasn't there when I drove past the next morning, or the one after that. Come to think of it, I never saw him again.

CHAPTER 6
THINGS TO TELL YOU

❝So, how did it acquit itself last night? What time did you arrive home?" My boss, Myles Ellison, inquired while dropping by my office around ten in the morning. Not that he really cared. Only he was politic enough to pretend he did. Then, he could fire off an email to our university's president with an embellished tale on how masterfully the situation had been handled. By *him*, it went without saying.

"About 3:30 in the morning. It took that long to break up the party, clear everyone out, and make sure one of their guys would be okay after being taken to the hospital." As dean of students at a massive school, it fell to me to take telephone calls 24/7 from campus police. With some exceptions—sexual assaults, weather events, accidental deaths—they mainly related to student parties which got out of hand and led to aggravated neighbors calling for help. Loud music blaring into the wee hours, beer bottles shattering on the street, the shouting of couples having a drunken quarrel, these comprised most of the complaints I fielded.

"Which house was it this time?" he asked me.

"Sigma Phi." From the expression on his face, I realized

that he didn't actually know the names of the active chapters on campus. There were twenty-four, but in staff meetings he railed about our twenty-seven problematic fraternities. It was a pattern for him. Although already vast in scale, Myles exaggerated the size of our student body and both the number and severity of crises our department, Student Affairs, handled. He presumed that in doing so, it rendered him even more valuable in the eyes of our president who had her own sights set on a promotion to the state Board of Regents. She didn't want those plans derailed by scandals. Which is why Myles and the services he provided mattered to her.

"They're an endangered species that we need to bring to extinction. All of these fraternities. We should shut them all down," he declared.

"It's a mixed bag, for sure. They cause us the most headaches when they misbehave and that's far too frequently. And yet, six of the last seven student body presidents have been Greek. More than 80 percent of the senators in student government are also affiliated. Ironic as it is, a majority of student leaders across this university hail Greeks. These organizations found the right formula to breed leaders. No other student organizations match their track record. Unfortunately, at least in that area, they seem to bring something worthwhile to our school."

"Bollocks. The only thing they breed are cretins. Overindulged children recreating their *nouveau riche* lifestyles here," Myles sneered. He often contrasted England's class structure with America's and invariably found a way to denigrate the Colonies. Campus gossipers put stock in a rumor that his father served in the House of Lords, that his offspring held hereditary titles of nobility, and that Myles did as well. For Myles to lower himself by working at all, much less at an upstart *American* university, implied this rumor was false. Not that it mattered. Wily as he was, Myles saved his sarcasms for those under him and—*viscount* or not—didn't direct them at his superiors.

"Why did you stay so late if it was just a regular party necessitating police intervention?"

"One of their brothers, Cosmo, mixed Xanax with vodka shots and blacked out. The others panicked when they couldn't wake him up. By the time I got on the scene with campus security, he was incoherent but partly conscious and moving a little. To be safe, I took the ambulance ride with him. He recovered at the hospital. I stayed until the parents made it down."

"Heroic of you." In truth, this was his job as vice president of campus life, but he delegated such duties to me when they fell outside of his regular 10 a.m. to 6 p.m. schedule. Let everyone else on staff do the unpleasant, late-night work while he held the top post and ingratiated himself with the higher-ups. It seemed like he didn't even like college students.

Oddly, whenever I did his job for him and did it well, he made extra efforts to needle me. Today was another opportunity. "It's important for you to be a smash with them, isn't it?" He watched to see if this barb made me defensive. It did not.

"Hardly. I wouldn't call what I did an attempt to be popular. It was just the right thing to do. To ensure no one was seriously hurt. Also, to remind the rest of them consequences were coming for breaking so many *Code of Conduct* rules."

"Ah, yes, I see. Yet even after you hold them accountable through a chapter suspension, a month or two from now they'll still invite you to speak at their Parents' Weekend Picnic or Founders' Day Dinner. Why is that?"

"Because they know me. And, I think, respect me."

"Is that all it is?" he said with thinly concealed contempt.

"Yes. That's all it is. They look to any adult who celebrates them when they do good things, for example, their annual food drive for the city's homeless shelters. And to anyone who also holds them responsible when they screw up, and is also willing to get them back on the right track."

"I am enlightened by your perspective. You have analyzed this issue thoroughly." Today he was nastier than usual. Perhaps it stemmed from a hangover. He made no secret of his fondness for imported scotch after hours.

"Myles, why'd you even get into student affairs if you disdain students so much?" Originating with my own weariness, I had my fill of his condescension.

"Careful, Tom. You have an annual contract and no security beyond the next twelve months. Mind your own affairs and don't concern yourself with mine. Send me a summary of what *we* did while intervening so I can share it with the president's office. Then head home and get some sleep. You look like excrement."

He walked out. I felt fine knowing I had done right by everyone concerned. Even him, though he would never admit it.

* * *

"Hey, Tom! Hurry up and come on in! Something amazing happened. I have to tell you about it." Alli waited just inside the door from our garage. She hopped with excitement as I closed my car door and walked toward her. Caught off guard by her levity, I replied, "Umm, okay. Great! But let me come inside and put my stuff down first. Then you can tell me." Still bouncing, she grabbed my hand, pulled me into the house, and led me to our kitchen table. "Sit in that chair," she commanded, but sweetly.

"Were you really in a seminar all day or do they just say that so no one can reach you?" Not waiting for my answer, she leapt ahead to her main purpose. "Are you ready to listen? Yes? Okay then ..." Trembling with anticipation, she needed to open the floodgates while everything was fresh.

* * *

This morning started darkly, another in a relentless string. Alli awoke with a heavy heart. Her daily fight not to dwell on the accident that took Mia away hadn't let up. Along with Nora, Gianni, and Katia, she blamed herself for not doing something, anything, to change the outcome of the fateful day. If only she had phoned Mia and spoken to her for two minutes, those precious seconds might have prevented her from being at the precise spot she was when the other car entered the intersection and hit her. Like the rest of the Ranna family, Alli was haunted by the what-ifs of this tragic situation. While she knew this kind of thinking led to a dead end of despair, it seemed impossible to avoid.

She stayed in bed staring at the ceiling, struggling not to fall back into the same trap. Wishing them away even harder, she closed her eyes. The mattress gave a little, as if someone sat down next to her. This sensation didn't make sense since she knew that I'd left for work hours ago. Eyes still shut, she extended her arm to where the bed sank. No one was there, of course. But her hunch that she wasn't alone didn't leave. It grew stronger. Her senses tingled, alerting her that someone else *was* there and almost touching her! A flash of recognition came into her mind—it was Mia!

But it couldn't be Mia ... Until she heard her sister's voice come through loud and clear in her head saying, oh, yes, it can be and is me! Mia thought-asked Alli why she didn't believe this

71

could be happening, when after all, hadn't she already visited us at the tavern and delivered a dessert we could appreciate? The brownie dessert convinced Alli then. Mia added that she had checked on her sister other times too.

Part of Alli wanted to face the spot where Mia seemed to be, but another part just could not. Fear prevented it. She worried about getting too emotional and breaking down into tears. If that happened, Mia might decide not to upset her further and leave. Besides, Alli didn't want to find that Mia wasn't actually there. All that would show was that she was going off the deep end.

Evidently, Mia could hear Alli's interior monologue and found her older sister's worry very entertaining. In between laughs, she told Alli to stop fretting. Yes, if it was true. This was really happening.

Mia explained why she came. She wanted my wife to stop anguishing. *It was holding her back.* It was also holding Alli back. Mia insisted that she was happy, whole and uninjured, and thriving in an indescribably wonderful place. Feeling the peace radiating from her, Alli had to agree that it must be incredible. Although urged to give more details, Mia wasn't allowed to say too much. Sensing confusion, she clarified. Mia was permitted to visit because of the abrupt transition from this life and because of the shock her family had absorbed. This is why she went to each of them—her mother, her father, her younger sister, and Alli.

She explained that when someone young died suddenly, exceptions might be granted to return to comfort the survivors. This is why she communicated with each of them in a way suited to that person's coping abilities. For one person it might be through a dream, while for another it might be a song coming on the radio they both liked. In her own case, Alli knew perfectly well what methods Mia used. Most of them were inside jokes which only the two of them understood and once laughed over. Mia was famous for her sense of humor. So, of course, she enjoyed playing silly but unique pranks on her serious older sister.

Although Mia hesitated to describe in detail her new home, Alli asked if she could at least tell her what she was doing there. Mia volunteered that she had important work to do. This is what held her back: her family's intense grieving and its emotional pull. She needed them to move on here, so she could there.

Checking to see if she still had my undivided attention, Alli paused, then said, "I'm going to paraphrase what Mia next said: Picture life on Earth as an elementary school for souls. Spiritually, everyone here is so young and in need of learning. Once we complete all the lessons at Earth-school, we move to higher level instruction in the next life. Make sense to you, Tom?"

Yes, I shook my head, so she continued.

There was one last thing Mia wanted to communicate. It was the prime reason she came. Today would be her last visit. Mia had stayed longer than normal to strengthen her relatives. However, there were things that could no longer wait. She begged Alli not to feel sad. She'd never be so far away that she couldn't give support if truly needed.

Upset at this news, Alli pleaded with her not to go. If Mia couldn't visit anymore, it would be ages before they talked or laughed again. Mia dismissed that view. Don't give the idea of it being "ages" before we're together again a second thought. Time was far different from what people imagined. A lifetime might seem long to us, but it was a blink of an eye where she was. They would be reunited in just a few minutes of universe time.

Alli felt the circle closing. Just before she left, Mia shared two insights. First, that the answers to all the questions Alli had about the next life would be answered one day and what she learned would explain everything. Second, she loved Alli and nothing could ever separate them for long. Especially since time didn't really even exist.

Alli concluded her story there. She returned to me, in the present, and our kitchen table. "Oh, Tom, with my heart so happy, I finally got brave enough to turn to the spot where I knew she'd been sitting. But too late. She wasn't there anymore."

"That's just like *them*, isn't it? Putting us in awe of their abilities." We smiled at the comparison.

If Alli's story ended, the lift it gave her didn't. Any ambiguity about the destination of her beloved sister was erased. She spoke to and felt the timeless love of Mia. In the wink of eternity's eye, they would be together again. Mia said so. Basking in the moment, we let our imaginations run with the glorious possibilities implied by our visitor.

It was Alli who broke our daydreaming. "Are you hungry? Dad called from the restaurant and said he made something special for us. Want to go?" Dad being Gianni, the "us" being she and I. Her appetite returning and her asking me to leave home to socialize were good signs. Signs of better times coming back to stay, I hoped.

"Yes, to both!" Among his considerable talents, Gianni was an amazing chef. He took pleasure in luring us to the café most every Friday night by creating delicious, not-on-the-menu, Italian dishes for us. Foodie that I was, it didn't take much coaxing to convince me. Best of all, dining with him would put a warm exclamation point on Alli's perfect day. Katia, the youngest sister, was coming too with the new boyfriend all of us were keen on meeting.

* * *

Predictably, the faculty meeting ran beyond its allotted time. This left me scrambling to get back to my office for a mentoring appointment with an undergraduate. Exiting the lecture hall, Dr. Rodney Montrose, a friend, motioned for me to wait. He wanted to walk out together and catch up in the minutes it would give us.

"Thomas! How is this grand experiment called life treating you? I haven't seen you at many university *soirees* lately. We've missed you and your lovely *inamorata*." Rodney taught medieval literature and his baroque manner of speech mirrored a passion for this courtly era. In some, this might be taken as pretentious. In him, it charmed. It was an unusual affair. As Rodney himself noted the day we met, "Who would think a man raised in inner-city Baltimore would fall crown over stirrups in love with Marlowe, Milton, or Shakespeare? However, I did. And I make no apologies for the infatuation." Fearless in this proclamation, I liked him immediately.

"I doubt, my friend, that my absences were much noticed. Now as for people missing my *paramour* ..." I played along with his antiquated style, "... that I can well believe." Alli did indeed light up every room she entered.

"Jesting aside, how is your enchanting consort? Losing her sister so young—twenty-four, was it—in an auto accident ... *Mon Dieux!* It had to be devastating. I can't even fathom such a grievous loss."

"Alli's still reeling, no question," I confirmed, "but also improving day by day. The visitations have helped her."

Whoops. An alarm sounded in my brain. What had I just done? The *visitations* have helped? A split-second lapse in my filtering mechanism and I blurt out the deepest of personal secrets. Way to go.

"What visitations? Visits from whom?" Rodney caught the slip. He pushed up the tortoise-shell glasses to the top of his nose and squinted at me, a habit which telegraphed him switching into full attention mode.

Regrouping after the error, I demurred, "It's nothing, Dr. Montrose." I came paper-thin close to revealing what happened at home these last few weeks. Rodney was the most trusted, open-minded friend I had at the university. Hearing from him that we weren't hallucinating would be a relief. Yet as much as I wanted to unburden myself, it remained a bridge too far. Even for the gentle and understanding person that he was. Cautiously I continued, but steered us in a different direction.

"Rodney, do you believe that people have ... souls?"

"*Souls*? I didn't see that coming, Thomas. Well, now, let me see. Since things have taken a turn from small talk into the metaphysical, allow me to collect my thoughts ... Well, I was raised African Methodist Episcopal and for all my years believed in what it taught even if my practicing of it has—how shall I say it?—waned. Therefore, yes, on your soul question. Why?"

"If yes, you must also believe in an afterlife. Otherwise, what would be the point of having a soul, correct?"

He ran a hand over his head but refrained from giving me a snap answer. Our friendship, based on lively debates, hinted I might be laying a philosophical trap. He didn't follow that I wasn't trying to trip him up. This time, it was a sincere interest in hearing his views.

To reassure him, I pressed ahead. "Rodney, I believe in God. Based on what you just said, is it safe to say you do as well?"

He nodded in the affirmative.

"I realize that makes us a rare breed around here. But it follows then, that we might house a piece of God in us—a spirit, if you will. Assuming we agree on this, do you think once someone dies, this divine fragment survives? And, just possibly, under the rarest of circumstances, it might conceivably return to ease a family's suffering?"

Lightning-quick, he jumped ahead to the only potential climax of our conversation. "You mean to say that your sister-in-law has *come back* to visit you? How exactly? Are you telling me you've actually seen her?" His eyes showed sympathy but the timbre of his voice didn't conceal the alarm. Given the worried expression on his face, I decided not to tell him that I hadn't just seen her but engaged in a dialogue about the next world.

"Nothing so dramatic," I fibbed. "There have just been some odd things occurring, coincidences, I suppose, that my wife thinks could only have originated with her sister. Random events, mind you, like receiving a free dessert at a restaurant that we never ordered but one which happened to be their mutual favorite. And ... this taking place while we were smack in the middle of remembering her lost sister. Or another time, where I had a dream about her coming to my home to do a welfare check on my ailing Alli." I lied again, because this was no dream.

"*Bravo!*" Rodney exhaled. "Dreams are subject to interpretation. And coincidences can be explained. Explained away, I mean." Not so fast. I pictured him crossing rhetorical swords with my eighth-grade-educated grandmother on the nature of coincidences and knew she would best him or any other learned person.

"Sightings, on the other hand, would spell trouble," Rodney asserted. "You have a bright future as a scholar as well as an administrator. Everything's unfolding nicely for you here. No one doubts you're on a fast track to the uppermost echelons. I'm not the only one who has heard your name come up as a candidate for the deanship once Chang re-retires."

Dr. Chang, my new supervisor, was brought in after Myles Ellison got promoted to the president's cabinet. Ken Chang was a kindly sort, but old, frail, and semiretired. Unfortunately, he was completely out of his depth in dealing with today's pleasure-preoccupied students. Our president appointed him as "interim" until a national search took place. The fact that the president hadn't named me as interim—an indicator of being in favor—showed the writing on the wall. Myles must have chirped uncharitable things about me in our leader's ear. This was a pattern for him to take down potential threats. I'd seen him do it before to others he wanted to keep at bay.

"Yes. I have a bright future here if I play politics and ingratiate myself with self-serving opportunists I cannot stand or respect."

We were in a throng of fellow professors, so Rodney gave me a disapproving look. "Lower your voice," he whispered. Pulling me aside, he held my elbow while waiting for the last stragglers to pass us. When they were outside of voice range, he started to lecture me. "Open your eyes, idealist! It's the way of the world, is it not? The worst people, who attained the summit by being ruthless and without conscience, run the machinery. The rest of us play our parts in the faint hope of somehow, someday succeeding them, then changing the status quo. You know this."

"This truth doesn't make it any easier for me to swallow."

"Regardless, you don't want to jeopardize your future by telling the equivalent of ghost stories to those here. Do so and kiss your career farewell." We had reached an archway outside the building's courtyard and beheld a panoramic view of the campus. Students were splayed out on the grass, some on their bellies reading books, others on their backs dozing under the sun.

We stopped. Rodney gave me a searching look. "I think of

you as a confidant as well as a gifted teacher. What I'm about to say comes from the friend but has ramifications for the professor. Mourn any way you see fit with Alessa and her family. *Les miserables*—those poor people. Acknowledge omens if they console you. Outsiders will concede such as part of the grieving process. Anything more … simply cannot be. People won't accept it. And word of it around here would brand you as unfit for higher office. After all, science vanquished faith in the academy some time ago." His statement saddened me because it was true. The earliest universities arose in the Middle Ages as extensions of the Church, reinforcers of faith through knowledge. How far they wandered over the last seven hundred years to become its enemy.

Still, I knew Rodney had my best interests in mind when he used both hands to shake mine good-bye. "Always a pleasure, Thomas. Let's take the noonday repast anon," he said with a flourish. Seeing my quizzical look, he translated. "Let's do lunch soon!" He hurried off his way. I went mine.

Our conversation drove home that experiencers of these events were the only ones with open minds. For intellectuals, a parallel reality which bore an inconvenient resemblance to "heaven," a debunked notion they mocked in proportion to the number of degrees held, was ludicrous. Only superstitious fools believed otherwise.

When Rodney categorically dismissed the idea, it hurt. Close as we had become, it was futile to try and change his mind. I had seen enough to know the cosmos was not an infinite, inanimate, indifferent sea. On the contrary, it was localized, alive, and aware of every individual's place in it.

Seeing my friend's inflexible attitude only hardened my own. No. I would keep these implausible events at home, where, apparently, they were meant to stay.

CHAPTER 7
DARKEST BEFORE DAWN

It was 6:40 a.m. on a flawless summer morning. Treetops caught the first rays of a stretching sun. Cicadas droned in unison and birds hidden among thick boughs chirped madly. Yet apart from this chorus, the world lay still. The clean, dewy air made the earth feel new. It was as if Creation finished only minutes ago.

With my cell phone in hand, I snapped a photo of the rays filtering through the branches and started texting it to Alli, but changed my mind. With the baby keeping her up at night, there was no cause to ping her. She could use the sleep. Besides, everything seemed so peaceful, I wanted to keep it all to myself.

While the world dreamt, I walked on the wet cobblestones of Alumni Way on the campus of a fabled university. Any year our football team didn't make, much less win, a major bowl game, or the basketball squad reach the Elite Eight, saw both students and alumni on the verge of rioting. Given the earliness of the hour, and that we were between academic sessions, no one was in sight. Alone with my thoughts on such a pristine morning, I should've been enjoying the quarter-mile walk from our parking garage to my office. Today, contentment was the farthest thing from what I felt.

For the last few months I hadn't been in a good place. Emotionally, I was running on empty. The smooth rhythms of my life had been upended. Five months ago, Alli and I became first-time parents. Our daughter arrived one day: fresh, beautiful, and wholly dependent the way all infants come. A seismic shift from *us* to *her* abruptly changed our cadence. In a flash, every day was consumed by diaper changes, feedings, baths, and fusses at naptime and bedtime. The bone-crushing weariness only new parents endure from perpetual sleep deprivation didn't improve my mood. Neither did skipping my trips to the gym and substituting them with a two-cocktail habit after work most nights. However, there was more to it.

I had been replaced. This plain truth rankled me. For twelve years of marriage, it had been Alli and me. Like most couples before children, the world had been our playground. We could afford stylish clothes and a home bigger than we needed, took vacations in the Caribbean, bought new cars, and indulged in the finer things. If this lifestyle seemed a luxury, what we treasured most was the time we set aside for our adventures. Travel, outdoor pursuits, concerts—any experiences done together—these gave us the greatest pleasure.

Then, a tiny, fragile being graced our household one day. Just like that, the couple's life that we loved ceased to exist. Yes, of course, we were euphoric about Camille. How could we not be? If a part of us wanted to cling to our former ways, the overwhelming part comprehended that things must change with the miraculous addition to our family. Alli seemed fine with it. She even sold the business she started ten years before and never regretted this choice. So what was wrong with me?

When I was being honest with myself, I knew the baby-introduced changes were not the real problem. Older friends told me the kids grow up fast and eventually move away. All those earlier indulgences, especially the best of them—time again, for you and your spouse—returned. But losing time with Alli wasn't my main gripe. No, it was a more primal impulse that plagued me. And its name was jealously. I resented my own daughter because her sudden presence eclipsed mine. With a few coos and cries, she became the apple of my wife's eye. Demoted, my new duties included breadwinner, protector, and father. These were noble. Unfortunately for me, my favorite role, husband to the most amazing woman on Earth, got downgraded so dramatically, it was as if it never existed.

Although my adult side accepted it had to be this way, the inner child in me refused. After more than a decade of marriage, I still wanted to leave work early to see Alli. Almost none of the freshness in our romance had worn off. She also felt enough of that giddiness to wait for me on the front porch most days. I would see her smile widen while turning into our driveway. She waved at me to hurry and park. On temperate afternoons, I loosened my tie, put down my briefcase, and sat down next to her on the steps while we talked. In colder months, we went inside and spent a couple of hours doing little more than just nagging out. Whatever the month on the calendar, we savored each other's company as much now as the two love-struck kids we once were. This was our fairy tale, twelve years strong and still going. Then it ended. I was angry about it.

Facing this fact made me feel horrible. What kind of person was jealous of his own child? True, none of my friends who achieved fatherhood before me had been honest about what to expect. To a man, they stuck to a script that required them to talk up its blisses while cleverly omitting its responsibilities. Immersed in these white lies, I simply wasn't prepared for the realities. For someone with a generous capacity to learn and adapt, this insecure, uglier side of my personality riddled me with guilt. I hated myself for feeling this way.

The office contributed to my unhappiness. To move up the ranks, you generally had to move to a new school, which I had done almost a year ago. As dean of students at one of the largest universities in the country, sacrifices were expected to fully commit to this job. In *theory*, this suited me fine since I loved the work itself. As students approached the threshold of adulthood, they wrestled with some of the biggest decisions of their lives. Many needed someone they could trust to talk over these weighty choices, from academic majors to career options. Intuitively, they knew that what they decided now would ultimately determine salaries, futures, and fulfillment. In *practice,* trying to balance this mammoth responsibility for fifty thousand students with my status as a new father was close to impossible.

We came home from the hospital with newborn Camille on Thursday. It was made clear, however, that I return to the office the following Monday or else. Duty didn't get set aside just because my first child arrived. Family Leave Act, university parenting policies, common decency, all be damned. Get back here or your job might not be. My new boss, embittered over his own domestic situation—a cheating ex-wife and adult sons who all moved away—held a grudge against anyone blessed with what he no longer had.

Needless to say, my "selfish" desire to spend a few dwindling hours of daylight with Camille before nightfall equated to a mortal sin. Always an early riser and the first one at the office, my ten-, twelve-, fourteen-hour workdays were still unsatisfactory. My supervisor told me so in the only negative performance review I ever received.

Prescience wasn't required to see how this would end. I didn't need to read the tea leaves to see that he would have no qualms about wrecking both my career and my family if I stayed. Unfortunately, the last thing I wanted to do was start a job search so soon. It made *me* appear suspect. Outsiders wouldn't know it was him instead of me. Praying my good work would gradually win him over, I stayed put. My wishful thinking proved to be a colossal mistake that would lead to a bad ending.

These were the jumble of discordant thoughts in my mind as I crossed the barren quadrangle. My jerk of a boss is determined to do me in. My wife, ever perceptive, can't help but see how juvenile I've been acting and probably hates me too for being so self-centered. I'm failing as a father, envious of my own precious daughter. I'd given up on going to church since my prayers never seemed to be answered. God sees how undeserving I am of any aid and left me to fend for myself, unsuccessfully. Most alarming of all, I sensed Alli's love pulling away from me. If it resulted from her maternal instincts assuming control, that was one thing. But if her withdrawal came from seeing me for what I really was these days, it terrified me. She was the one constant of unwavering light and love in my otherwise tumultuous life.

No, it could not get any worse. It did, though, a second later when I tripped on an uneven cobble and fell to my knees. Where they hit on the rough stony surface made a hairline tear in trousers of a suit I was wearing for the first time. Par for the course.

"*I despise myself.*" There, I confessed it out loud after completing a turn to make sure no one else was near on this wide avenue. Nor would I blame the universe and everything in it for hating me either.

* * *

Utterly defeated, I brushed the dew stain off my knee and resumed walking. Moments later, I heard an echo of footsteps behind me. This couldn't be. I just scanned for other people and no one else was in sight. Perplexed, I cast a backward glance over my shoulder. It was a young woman approximately fifteen feet behind and closing. She must be one of our students.

How had she gotten this close and so quickly? More than that, where did she come from? I had just turned a full circle in surveying the area and had not observed another human being. There were no classes currently in session. The campus was practically deserted. What in the world would the girl be doing up and strolling about before seven in the morning? This was hardly prime time for the college set and it was rare to see any student out at this hour unless they were baristas headed to the local coffee shops. However, a clustering of such shops was on the other side of this city-sized campus, and in the opposite direction that we were going. Besides, she wasn't sporting the Starbucks, Coffee Beanery, or Jada's Morning Joe uniforms. She seemed to have dropped silently out of the sky.

Unnerved, I continued walking. As I did, the girl's pace seemed to quicken. What was she up to? Trying to close the distance between us? Time to end the mystery. I stopped in my tracks and turned to assess her intentions. Like a reflection, she also stopped, faced me from five feet away.

We studied each other. Traces of a smile played along her mouth. A colorful bandana encircled and held her hair in place. There was a large tattoo on her neck ending at her jawline. A series of exotic symbols were the mainstay of her body art.

Although I couldn't identify them as either glyphs or letters, something inside me said they were very ancient. An idea about their meaning—*Aramaic*—coalesced in my mind, but I had no frame of reference to compare it against her body art. Despite these esoteric symbols, the rest of her appearance was consistent with other college students. She lugged a fat backpack over one shoulder. In her other hand, she balanced a Starbucks cup. Given this ensemble, it had to be one of our students.

Considering we were total strangers, it struck me as odd that she exhibited no shyness. This was the Midwest and adolescents still showed an exaggerated politeness toward adults they didn't know. From the way she regarded me, I guessed that she was pondering how to open a conversation with someone not as readily inclined. Then a smile took charge of her face. It was extraordinary, of a kind I had not seen before. She drew closer, slowly extended her hand to hold my elbow and keep me in place. Something significant was coming. The girl wanted to make sure my attention was riveted on what came next.

"*God loves you so*," she said assuredly, with a hint of a Jamaican accent. Despite the sanctity of these words, she delivered them proudly and without hesitation.

"Excuse me?" I stammered. Shocked by what she said and her fearlessness in saying it, I hardly believed my ears. *What did she just say to me? Who talks like that? To a total stranger? Where did she come from, anyway? I didn't see anyone a few minutes ago. And why did she approach me?*

"I'm sorry. I don't think I heard you correctly. What did you say?"

"*God loves you so*," she repeated. "Leave the dark place you're in behind. Those self-destructive thoughts too. *He understands you.* He sees the important work you're doing with them. The students." Unusual phrasing in selecting *them* instead of *us*. Although she dressed the part of a student, the girl distanced herself. *"He sees you. In all your faults. In all your strengths. He loves you,* no matter what. Don't doubt it, or lose hope.*"* She let go of my arm and stepped backward. The wattage of her incandescent smile increased, making her entire person shimmer.

How in the world would a twenty-something I didn't know gain access to my private thoughts? The emotional penetration rattled me. "Hold on! Who are you? Have we met before?"

"Not like this," came her unexpected reply. Was that a no? A yes? Both? Neither?

"'Not like this?' What in the heck does that mean?"

"We know each other. From before. But not like this."

"No, you're mistaken. We've definitely not met before! I'd remember you. Tell me, please, what's your name?" I pushed. The more agitated I became, the calmer her demeanor.

"Arielle," she spoke, accenting the last syllable and giving it a majestic flair to match her persona. "If that means anything to you," she added, sympathetically, as though all of what had unfolded ought to be clear to me.

Rattled, I lost my grip on the cell phone in my hand. Swinging to catch it in midair made things worse and I knocked it even farther away from where it would have landed at my feet. The device clattered on the cobblestones and in the still morning air, the impact cracked like a rifle shot and echoed around the empty quad. Embarrassed, I rushed to where it came to rest.

Steps later, I bent over to pick it up. Recovering my cool, my next question was ready for firing. Whirling around, I demanded, "So *who exactly* are you …?"

One problem: I was suddenly alone again. She vanished the same way she arrived. Into thin air.

Frantically, I whirled around and checked the landscape in every direction. The nearest building to me, our student union, stared indifferently from a hundred yards away. Other buildings, unmolested and unpeopled, behaved the same. It was inconceivable this girl could have covered so much ground in the mere seconds I wasn't watching her. Arielle had been right there next to me. Then she was not.

In that instant, the world paused. The sun's rising, hands on my wristwatch, ambient sound, all came to a full stop. A wave of warmth swelled in the middle of my body. It rose up and washed over me. *God loves you so.* Words my ailing heart needed to hear. A thought also crested on this wave.

In spite of the college student appearance, maybe this girl originated from somewhere farther away than the West Indies. Everything about her suggested it.

The warmth within ebbed. Aware now that I was holding my breath when the tide engulfed me, I finally exhaled. Time resumed its flow. Nature re-animated. Sighing, I took a step toward my building. On the rise of a hill, it was the only one with any sign of activity—while I watched, someone opened the window blinds in my office suite and switched on the lights.

I wasn't a lost cause. Surely there would be a slew of days that I didn't measure up. Other days might be better. But even those times when I stumbled, someone upstairs would still care about me.

* * *

Not like this. It was how the girl, Arielle, demurred when asked if we had previously met. What did her enigmatic answer mean? These emissaries didn't mince words. Everything they verbalized or thought-said was carefully chosen to achieve a desired effect. Her remark wasn't offhanded. *Not like this.* How, then?

My memory strained to associate her to a recent university event. There were so many at an institution our size. I racked my brain, poring over a parade of banquets, symposia, recitals, athletic contests across sports and seasons, yet still came up blank. No one her age showed the poise and wisdom that she did. Or displayed her prescience in knowing what I was thinking about. Another strangeness, no one I met at this state university invoked the name of God when opening conversation with a stranger. Doing so would constitute an almost incomprehensible breach of social decorum. No, I would have admired and remembered the courage of such a student.

A memory stirred. Maybe there *was* another time. When my being reacted the same way as it did when the girl left. The time, place, and circumstances were so very far away, yet the similarities were inescapable. When I was almost nine and nearly drowned, Lizabeth intervened. She rescued me from a life-threatening situation. This morning was another kind of saving. I was spared from an equally dire situation. Only it was my mind and spirit hanging in the balance instead of my body. Lizabeth, then, Arielle, today?

Were they one and the same? Lizabeth declared that she had been with me since *the before time* and would always remain near. Then I never saw her again. This morning, Arielle referenced us knowing each other from *before*. Was she connecting the dots for me?

Fast forward these years to a different stage of my life, update the setting to my present circumstances, and the possibility didn't seem so far-fetched. Although neither of them stated it, if Lizabeth or Arielle issued from heaven, they, *she*, might appear in any form desired to deliver the timeliest of messages.

After all, inexplicable incidents had become commonplace in my otherwise predictable world. Perhaps Arielle came to me, the man, to reinforce a pledge that Lizabeth made to me as a boy. It consoled me to know that she—this one being—stayed near. Just as she promised me never to fail me when I was a little kid.

* * *

Camille chattered madly away as I held her in my arms that night. She was regaling me with news of her day in a language mysterious to all but her. Yet the rapid-fire jauntiness of her speech made it plain she was happy. If I could only decipher the story she was excitedly telling me.

After caring for her all day, Alli was tired by evening. Before putting Cami down for the night, it was my turn. Happy days or bad, and there had been more of the latter lately, I looked forward to our bonding time. The intensity of my day melted away whenever I cradled her. Tonight, she seemed extra talkative.

What a miracle she was. Exquisitely formed, her tiny hand barely filled a quarter of my palm. Her hair felt like silk to the touch. Her skin was flawlessly smooth and unblemished. Her breath, even after the formula-feeding, somehow smelled fresh and clean. My wife's colorful description of our daughter: Cami was a newly minted human being right off heaven's assembly line. Needless to say, a soiled diaper might temporarily wreck this illusion, but tidied up, it didn't take long for the certainty that Camille was made of stardust to return.

Holding my daughter, I imagined her future. What kind of little girl would she be? Sweet, social, and kind, I hoped. The type who would be the first to say hello to the new kid in class or stand up to a playground bully. How would her tumultuous teenage years turn out? With us close by, would she be strong enough to hold her own against the siren song of popular culture and temptations it dangled but never the consequences? Then, much further ahead … what kind of woman would she be? Caring, compassionate, ethical? A doctor or lawyer or teacher? A wife, mother, career woman, all three? Time would tell.

Camille had her own destiny. We would be there to give her guidance, support, and love at every step. Eventually, though, she would have to stand on her own two feet, rely on her internal compass, and make her own decisions. Our parenting work would be done. If we'd done it well, Alli and I would see her as our greatest accomplishment. And justifiably, we would share a tremendous sense of pride.

With the fresh start an offbeat college student provided me earlier in the day, I forgave myself for being a million miles short of perfect. That girl reminded me that come what may, God was there to shore me up just like I would for my child. The symmetry of it wasn't lost on me.

Camille expelled a loud burp, which startled even her, but the only odor in it was sweetness. I continued rocking her in my arms. Alli entered the nursery to say, "It's time, Tom. Let's lay her down in the crib." Even though the minute she touched the mattress, Cam often perked up and fussed, tonight it didn't matter. The scene was too beautiful to ruin.

Alli had an impromptu change of heart. "Wait a sec. Hand her over. I want a little lovin' too." They snuggled and made funny little sounds together. Watching, I was smitten with both of them. In my heart, I thanked Arielle for giving me the perspective to see clearly again.

CHAPTER 8
FATHERS AND SONS

Reclining in a lounge chair on the covered patio of my house, I listened to raindrops tapping a mellow cadence on the tin roof above me. My breathing slowed to match its lazy rhythm and my mind also wandered into the calm. Sunday afternoons, far from the madding crowd, were made for such interludes.

Admiring the nicely manicured lawn of my backyard and row of towering cedars marking the property line, the scene rippled. Seconds later, it rippled again. This rippling effect was something altogether new. Over the last couple of months, from out of the blue, I might notice a wave roil my surroundings. It passed in mere seconds and was always solitary. The wave mostly came when I was in a pensive mood, after an arduous day at the office, and as I shed all the people, conversations, and tensions of previous hours. In spite of its weirdness, the phenomenon didn't worry me. To my thinking, its source was emotional fatigue.

Another ripple in the fabric of this scene, the longest yet, distorted my view. When it cleared, a different landscape sharpened into focus. In it, a weary sun languished above the horizon. Pink and orange streamers of light danced on the sea in front of me. I sat alone on a salt-bleached dock not long before sunset. My home, patio, and their familiar feel disappeared. I had been taken somewhere else. Or perhaps I hadn't really traveled anywhere. Realities had a strange tendency of merging in my life but didn't announce when they did.

This world seemed constructed of a more ornate substance. Everything within eyesight, from the weathered wood planks under me to the white-topped waves, to the marsh grass swaying above the dunes, throbbed with energy. It seemed each particle of matter here was self-aware and trembling with joy. I picked up on a sound too. There was a pitch to the pulsing. It was a soothing tone that seemed to match a frequency inside me I didn't know was there.

Iridescent colors spread throughout the sky, so alive they made those of home pale in comparison. Beside myself with awe, I sat still so as not to alter any nuance of this glorious place.

One more ripple. Subtle but very much felt, it altered the pitch of this scene. I looked toward where the ripple started, toward whatever interloped. What ... no way. It was my father. He walked nearer and sat down on the pier next to me. Our legs dangled over the edge of the boards, casting long shadows on the water underneath. He smiled at me, then turned to face the surreal beauty in front of us.

Bathed in amber light, I noticed he was young again. Signs of old age no longer touched him. He looked to be in his prime, around thirty-five. The gray in his hair was gone, replaced by its original auburn. Or was this only a trick of the ebbing light?

In disbelief, I stammered out, "Is it really you, Dad?"

"Yes, Tom. Who else would it be?" he quipped, bright blue eyes twinkling again. While taciturn by nature, he always enjoyed wordplay with me just as I remembered.

"How is this possible? You're, uh … not alive anymore." Although he died six years earlier, I couldn't bring myself to say *dead.* It sounded too cold, too clinical, too final. Nor did I want to apply so permanent a term to my father. Especially when he clearly had not ended and was seated beside me.

"From your point of view, yes. On the other hand, where I am, I couldn't be more alive," he said, matter-of-factly. "Death isn't what you think. Not at all what you think," he emphasized …

* * *

There just wasn't enough time. To bring it to where I felt satisfied with things between us. Like so many fathers and sons, our relationship went through seasons. Some were rich while others were lean and left us hungry. Perhaps that was always the way of it with men and their male offspring. Although I didn't tell him this to his face, my father was a great man. Not necessarily in the ways the world measures greatness, but in those that counted most.

He and my mother stayed together for fifty-two years and he had stars in his eyes for her until the very end. Once, he shared a secret about their relationship which accounted for its longevity. By this time, he had retired and lost a step, explaining the looser tongue when it concerned what was proper for casual conversation versus information better kept private. This disclosure happened on an after-dinner walk. I complimented him on their coming anniversary and what a monumental milestone it would be. In a touching moment, Dad revealed that my mother was the only woman he had ever loved and how no one else on Earth could compare. It's possible his declaration might be interpreted in more than one way, but I took it literally: that he found his soul mate in her. What I cherished even more about this intimation was him adding that he'd go to his grave certain of their bond. Fidelity to those he loved defined him.

With us, his children, Dad chose a middle ground between meddling and giving us the freedom to be ourselves. There were rules, but fair and not strictly enforced. Reason became his default tool for dealing with misbehavior, even when we really pushed the limits. At fifteen, I once snuck his car out for a joy ride while only having a learner's permit. Rather than getting grounded or berated, he sat me down for an epic question-and-answer session to point out the dozen flaws in taking such a risk. He went over the disastrous outcomes that might have occurred and how they would have been my responsibility alone. "I am so *disappointed* in you, Tom," he said, dealing me a death blow in this intellectual grilling. Feeling his intense dismay, I swore not to do anything so harebrained again. None of us wanted to let him down. We dreaded any opportunity we gave him to drop the "D" word on us.

Faith was another yardstick to measure him by. He didn't miss church on Sunday. Dad believed in God, the Holy Church, and how the Almighty had created something magnificent in the United States of America. Don't ever lose faith in the Lord, or this great country, he repeated a million times to us growing up. For those who stayed strong, God would provide.

Not long after he died, me and Alli went home to help Mom go through his personal belongings. Alli sifted through a vast collection of ancestry files. He dedicated years to learning more about our family line. By right, it should have fallen to me as his namesake. But I was still too sad to close the book on his life by rummaging through his most prized possession. Our family tree meant a great deal to him. He took pride in our ancestors, their courage to migrate here, and the struggles they endured—generations of coal miners who died young from black lung, railroad men, and right before him, automotive workers—so that he and his children could be better off.

In a folder of papers, Alli stumbled across a note addressed to me. It was titled, *Prayer for Tom*. He never mentioned it to Mom or me, yet it was written in his own hand ten years ago, according to the date at the top. The note implored me to stand firm in the Catholic pedigree of our Irish ancestors. Certainly, hardships awaited me on my journey through life, as it had prior generations. If I honored my heritage, however, he believed that the rewards in heaven would be worth it.

Moved by his words, I kept this piece of wisdom in a safe place, regarding it as the second most precious of my inheritances. The safe place was our family Bible. When I was little, I watched him pore over it many times, jotting notes in the margins. On my twenty-fifth birthday, he gave it to me, his son, as guardian of the Connor bloodline. Feigning enthusiasm, I thanked him and then tucked it away in a bin in my basement. Twenty-five was the year I felt least tied to religion or even tradition. Fortunately, I rediscovered it while rummaging through these dust-covered bins just short of my thirty-seventh birthday. I inserted into this most precious of things bequeathed me, the *Prayer for Tom* that he committed to paper and pen.

To relatives and friends, my father died before his time. He suffered complications after a routine surgical procedure. A month after returning home, he suffered a heart attack. Mom said that he was gone before he hit the floor.

Unlike everyone else, I wasn't so sure Dad died too soon. With his convictions, he was always prepared. He viewed death as a homecoming. I saw how much he missed his own parents, brothers, and sister, all of whom had already passed on. Of course, he still loved life and seeing his children grow into respectable adults, spouses, and parents who cherished our own families as much as he and Mom did us. They often said that we were their greatest achievement.

Flashback to the last holiday season before we lost him. Me, Alli, and nearly two-year-old Camille were visiting my parents' house. Flat on my back on the carpet, with the Christmas tree blazingly lit in one corner and the television playing *A Charlie Brown Christmas* in the other, I held Cami between outstretched arms. At regular intervals, I emitted a whoop, tossed her up an inch or two, then deftly caught her an instant later. She giggled with delight during the split-second of free falling. The louder my whoops got, the wilder her giggling became. Dad watched from his chair.

"Hey, Tommy ..." I heard him say between peals of our laughter. Whoops. We'd gotten carried away. He was right to tell us to shush so he could hear the television set again. From my childhood, I remembered how he looked forward to the segment where Linus explains the true meaning of Christmas to Charlie Brown. It was always my favorite part too. So, I stopped our gymnastics to watch the scene with him. Camille, not knowing why her raucous fun ended, pouted and fidgeted.

"Sorry, Dad. Guess we were having way too much fun," I apologized. Sitting up, I placed Cami on my lap and glanced over at him. His eyes were moist. They moved between my daughter and me. "Look at you," he spoke, in a voice quivering with emotion. "The way you play with her. Laugh with her. Love her ..." Another tremor ran through his speech and he halted until it passed. Clearing his throat, he made a remark that I would later treasure. "Like the father I always wanted to be with you when you were that small."

My father rarely wore his heart on his sleeve. He came from a generation of men stronger than mine and it molded him. Boys born after World War II were raised by their soldier-fathers to be hard-working, uncomplaining, no-nonsense, and unsentimental. Mom admitted that he didn't change our diapers, bathe, or coddle us when we were infants. He all but confirmed it when he told me once that he didn't find us especially interesting until my sisters and I started talking. But neither did Dad play at being too tough. Underneath his tranquil exterior, I detected a deep reservoir of feeling. That he loved his children was evident from the thousand times he helped with homework, listened to our problems, included us in his hobbies, and provided us a carefree upper-middle-class life. If there was one hurdle he had to overcome, it was his discomfort at displaying public affection. Knowing the era that birthed him, this didn't bother me. Presuming his own father was even less demonstrative with him, I was proud of how many miles he came on his own.

* * *

"… If death isn't what I think, then what is it?"

"A doorway into worlds you can't even imagine, which you'll discover when we're together again."

"You're saying that we'll all be together again someday?"

"Of course. Everyone in our family. Alli's too, along with anyone you cared about or who cared about you. Be patient. It will become clear to you. For now, you just have to wait." He meant this to reassure, but there was a line he would not cross. In what they stated as well as where they stopped, I had picked up on this boundary thing. Lizabeth, Mia, Arielle, now my father—they only went so far in pulling back the curtain. We mortals not knowing too much about what lay ahead must be foundational to the celestial order.

"Did it hurt? To die? That day in the kitchen with Mom?"

"No time to notice. I passed over in an instant. Then … I was somewhere else."

"Heaven?"

He smiled, nodding so slightly it was almost imperceptible. What Dad didn't do was say, definitively, yes, I found myself in heaven. Intrigued by this omission but certain he wouldn't budge on subjects not predetermined—these visitors addressed only what they were sent to do and what you most needed—I changed topics.

"Man, have I missed you." Though five simple words, I still felt the loss in every cell of my being. There was so much ground that we never covered together. Before I drew upon a tenth of his wisdom, my father was gone.

"I know, son. I miss you too." He spoke with compassion but no pity. The words sprang from a deeper well. I had noticed this before too. Feelings weren't the same over there. Here, healthy emotions such as loyalty or selflessness brought out the best in people. Negative ones like anger or envy evoked the worst. From my encounters, I gathered it was intellect instead of emotion which powered their words. They didn't need sentimentality like we did. They had no need since there was no desire to flatter, or belittle, or manipulate. Without such emotional priming, communication was much purer.

But if they had evolved so far as to leave intense feeling behind, I wasn't as advanced. Hearing my father say that he missed me triggered something I'd been carrying with me a very long time. A dam burst inside.

"Then why did you wait so long to visit me? You left *six years* ago. All the while I kept waiting. That you would come to me in a dream or show up like Mia did after she died. She returned several times. You … not once. *Why?*" My blood still boiled at this seeming abandonment.

"Slow down," he said, unfazed by my outburst. "You've said a lot. First, Mia's situation wasn't mine. I lived a full life. She didn't—at least in the sense it seems to you or Alli. Because you were in such despair, there was an urgency to her making contact. She needed to lead you out of the darkness. For me, it wasn't the same. Second, time is different where I am. Past, present, future … they aren't real. All of them are right now. It's impossible to explain. You can't comprehend, until you experience it."

That time issue resurfaced yet again. "I know, I know. Mia mentioned something similar." Her comments to Alli about time led me to do some research. I was startled to learn that modern quantum physics supported a view that time was not linear as people thought. Einstein called our belief in a distinct past, present, and future one "stubbornly persistent illusion." Mia and Dad echoed this notion, but unlike scholars only theorizing, they might actually know.

"Then you should have listened to her. Mia is a wise spirit." He praised her as if they were well acquainted when they only exchanged pleasantries a handful of times during Connor-Ranna holiday gatherings.

I arrived at my main gripe. "It hurt me, Dad. It really hurt. I'm your one son. I love you and thought you felt the same about me. After you left, died, I had no one to confide in, no one for guidance, nowhere to turn when I needed wisdom. I couldn't believe you didn't try to connect with me."

How my father answered left me gasping for intellectual breath ...

* * *

At his funeral, I delivered the eulogy. Mom couldn't. My sisters were relieved that my comfort level giving lectures to auditoriums full of students exempted them from this sad duty. Still, I was also reeling from his sudden death and proceeded vacantly through the rituals encircling it. Which is why I don't remember much of what I spoke about to the congregation.

One thing I did recall was my father including me in his own interests. I told them how when I was a boy he let me stay up past my bedtime to watch *Star Trek* with him. We admired the intrepid Captain Kirk and enjoyed watching him and the *Enterprise* warp around the galaxy on endless adventures. The show got us so enthused about astronomy that Dad made flash cards of every major constellation. Together, we memorized them—Orion, Lyre, Ursa Major, and more—and then tested each other's knowledge to see if we mastered our studies. Seeing him, in my mind's eye, beam with pride when I finally got them all correct, choked me up.

Standing on a pulpit in front of over a hundred people, I couldn't find my voice. Seconds ticked like minutes. I was frozen. At the very moment panic set in, Camille wrenched free of her mother's grip and came tearing down the main aisle of the church. Her jubilant cries of "Hi, Daddy! Can I come up there too?" shattered the heaviness. The assembly broke into peals of laughter. I didn't doubt for a minute it was my father who sent her running to the altar. It was just his style. He didn't dwell on sad things while alive, and from the afterlife, wanted to sweep away

101

the melancholy mood.

If his passing created a void these days, this wasn't always the case. Rifts between us weren't uncommon. A big one started at fourteen when I quit playing competitive baseball to switch to track. He was crazy for baseball, so naturally, I decided to spurn it. We hardly spoke for a month after I informed him of my decision. This marked the beginning of our estrangement and it lingered, through other areas of disagreement, for years.

I disappointed him a little when I passed on law school to pursue a graduate degree in psychology. In his estimation, having a lawyer-son would demonstrate the ascent of our family line. My spoiling this aspiration stung him. It was only after becoming a father myself did I appreciate how every parent wanted their child to do better than they did.

I disappointed him a lot when in the middle of my doctoral research, we argued about God's role in human affairs. I argued that *if there was a God*, he had made a mess of history. There was no doubt these words would hurt him. Faith played a massive part in Dad's life. When I made the remark, which I didn't really believe, it sent a message that I had my own views and wouldn't blindly follow his anymore. All sons eventually stepped out from their fathers' shadow. But I chose my topic and timed my breakaway for maximum effect. After the dust settled from this quarrel, we remained civil to each other for the family's sake. But it drove a wedge between us which did not mend itself for a few years.

In retrospect, I understood that all he wanted for me—in school, career, moral matters, and family—was not to settle for less than my best. If I did this, success would surely find me.

Fortunately, there was one place where I didn't let him down. It was in my choice of partner. He adored Alli.

Not long after we married, Dad was forced into early retirement by his company. They went on a youth drive and he was an old-timer. Freed, he planned to enjoy leisurely days with the wife, kids, and grandkids. With hours to spare at last, he made a point of calling my house punctually once a week to hear the latest news. Ironically, as he was reclaiming his life and the hours in it, I was ceding control of mine to the rat race. With me working long hours and seldom at home, he spoke to Alli when he phoned. From what she said, they talked for at least an hour most occasions. Much of their conversations centered on me.

I smiled at this revelation. True to form, it was my father's subtle method of staying connected to me. Alli became the bridge between us.

* * *

"… I can see what's happening in your life," Dad resumed. "This is why I know that you don't need me like you once did." He ran a finger along the grain of the wood planking we sat upon. At once, I disagreed.

"Yes, I do. What person wouldn't want his or her father to be part of their life, no matter how old they are?"

"Wanting is one thing, needing is different. You don't need me anymore, Tom. I look to see how you're getting along. I can see how you are with your lovely wife and daughter. I can also *feel* how *they feel* about you. Alli loves how much you care for, provide for, and protect them. Camille idolizes you. Those college students that you mentor, and actually listen to, when other adults pretend, also think the world of you. They need role models. If only you could see the long-term impact you've had on so many people the way that I can."

Gratifying though it was to hear this, I hadn't finished complaining. "I'm not that wonderful. Check with Alli or Camille when I'm having a bad day. There is so much I still get wrong. Which is why I wish you were still around to advise me."

He dismissed my last comment.

"All of us are works in progress. It doesn't stop either, where you are or where I am. Don't be too hard on yourself. Don't get frustrated if it takes time to improve. You have infinity."

"Is that what heaven is? Limitless opportunities to learn and get it right?" I put it to him. He flipped the viewing lens, then responded.

"What greater pleasure would any father have than seeing his children continue to grow in wisdom and love and service?" I knew right then that he was talking about God.

My father stood up and squinted at the last rays of sunlight dancing like diamonds on the water. "I have to go." I pleaded with him to stay but knew it was futile. A sharpness defined beginnings and endings in these encounters. Regardless, there was one item of unfinished business that had to be resolved.

"Wait one more minute. Before you go, I want to apologize for something. It's hung over my head since high school and I'm desperate to make amends. It's this: I'm really sorry for bailing out on baseball. You put so much of yourself into developing my skill. Then, when I was fourteen, it all came together. I played my best season and made the district all-star team. High schools across Ohio started to recruit me. You were thrilled. It wasn't long after the season ended I told you that I wouldn't be playing anymore. I can still see the shock on your face. It nags at me even now. It was an awful, selfish thing to do. I could've handled it so much better. I've been waiting to tell you how wrong it was."

"Tommy, Tommy, Tommy ..." he began, using my name

in a manner he seldom had, except when he wanted to convey affection. *"It's all right.* You liked running more and put your heart into it. Baseball became a grind to you. I realized it once you stopped playing. No, it was me who kept pushing it. I had the blinders on, not you. I'm the one who should be apologizing. For making you pursue a sport you didn't love anymore and keeping you away from one you did. I should have seen things more clearly than I did."

"Then you're not mad at me?"

"For doing what you loved? No. I'm proud of you for standing your ground and choosing your own road. Taking your own direction instead of mine was something you were courageous enough to do. From the time you were little until now, you've never struggled with finding your path. Not many people have that strength. You were born with it. I didn't recognize it then but I see it clearly now."

"Thanks, Dad. It's good to hear that you weren't holding any grudges for my idiotic teen behavior."

"There's no grudge-holding here. Besides, why would I ever hold one against my boy? Doing that holds me up too." Standing tall, he scanned the horizon, then faced me. This interlude was nearly up.

"Will you come back again?"

"No, I won't. We don't need to talk again. You became the man I always prayed you would become. I couldn't be prouder. Our agreement's been fulfilled."

"Agreement?" What agreement did he mean?

"The one we made, before. Add it to the list of 'you will understand, someday.' By the way, keep loving your wife. She's one in a million. And that daughter of yours? If you saw how luminous her spirit is ... oh my word! God truly loves you to have given you them to experience life with. Oh, and one last thing. *I love you, Tom.*"

My mouth formed a protest that he shouldn't go but nothing came out. While I watched, my father became transparent until he wasn't there with me anymore. I closed my eyes, absorbed the sun's diminishing warmth as it dropped to the horizon, and meditated on this final act in our relationship. I don't know how much time elapsed, if such a thing even existed. When I opened my eyes, I was back on the patio, listening to the rainfall.

Dad kept his word. He moved on to whatever came next for him. After this reunion, I didn't see him again. He said it would be that way. There were no more loose ends to tie up. We were both content.

Alli poked her head out the sliding glass doors.

"Did you fall asleep? I know how much you like the white noise in nature and how it relaxes you."

"I don't know. I don't think so." Which was true. It had a very different quality than a dream. Also, my dreams didn't begin with the ripple effect.

"Anyway, sorry to interrupt your rest. Wanted to tell you that your mom called. She's a little blue and asked that you return her call. Today would have been your dad's birthday. She said that you are the next best thing and if she can't speak with him, you're next in line."

"Be right in, love. Thanks for relaying the message." Dad came to me to make things right between me and him. Now it was my turn to make things as right as I could for someone who loved him even more than me.

My father's name was Ryan. Had I told you that? He wasn't perfect. But a finer man, I've never known.

CHAPTER 9
THE FLOWER LADY

The door to her bedroom was ajar. From the hallway, I heard Camille rustling under the blankets. Every morning, she waited for Alli or me to come in and start her day properly. If normal four-year-olds slept like stones, ours did not. From the day we brought her home, she hadn't kept her eyes shut more than a few hours at a time. By a year, she dispensed with the afternoon naps. My daughter was born with a restless energy and curiosity to match. This is how she managed to be so shiny each morning.

I pushed the door open, gently, in case she wasn't fully awake. My hope was to steal some precious seconds to watch her sleep. There was something irresistible about the way she looked while sleeping: it made her appear more angelic and beautiful than she already was. Good—she wasn't already standing there and waiting for me!

Tiptoeing further in, I scored a few fleeting moments to study her and her bedroom. Cami had been in her "big girl bed" since the age of two. It was adorned by a thick comforter with tiny pink ponies prancing over its surface. A painted white bedframe matched the large dresser whose upper shelves were filled with smiling stuffed animals. Photos from her earliest life adventures, all Firsts—at the beach, ballet class, riding a horse, preschool pageants—dominated a lower shelf. Somehow, she found my old Hot Wheels car collection in a seldom-opened closet and picked three of the "prettiest cars" from it to intersperse among her First photos, a direct tribute to the favorite and main male presence in her life. Feminine and whimsical, the décor could not be more perfect for a little girl's bedroom, courtesy of my thoughtful wife.

Despite my soft footsteps, all caution had been unnecessary. Peeking out from her downy burrow under the quilt, letting her eyes adjust to be sure it was me, Camille flung off the covers and jumped up. Part of our morning ritual, she waited for a hug. "Daddy? Daddy! Hi! It's you today. Yay! What day is it?" A child learns the world through routines and the fact that this morning I greeted her rather than her mother was a wrinkle she picked up on immediately.

"It's Saturday, little darling. It's the weekend. You know what that means? I get to spend the whole day with you and Mommy! Yay, is right!" Lifting her up, we cuddled. When I put her back down on the bed, she switched to a serious tone.

"Hey! There's something I have to tell you. I met the Flower Lady after I woke up today. We played together. She was nice! You know her too, right?"

"Oh, so you've been up for a while already?" I asked, hardly surprised by the news. "Wow, that's cool, Cami. But no, I don't think I ever met the Flower Lady." At four, I assumed she was blurring the line between a happy dream and real life. "Anyway, what did you two do together?"

"Well ..." she began coyly, "part of it is kind of a secret. She didn't say it had to be but I kinda' feel like it should. The first part isn't secret though. I can tell you about that," Cami decided.

"Whatever you want, lovebug. Tell me the non-secret part, then."

"Okay. Me and her played a fun game. She showed me a picture of a flower and I had to guess the name. The first one she showed was easy. I got it right away. A rose! You know how I knew? Because it was the same kind you give Mommy on her birthday. Neat that I remembered that, huh?"

"You bet it is. That's impressive, sweetheart." I held up my hand and we high-fived. "What happened next?"

"Well … then the Flower Lady showed me a daisy. And I didn't even have to guess 'cuz I knew that one right away too. Daisies grow in our yard, 'the wild ones,' I heard you and mommy say before. At first you guys said they were weeds but then you changed your minds and called 'em wild daisies. They make our yard look pretty, which is why you didn't weed-whack them down. Right?"

"Amazing. You're on a roll, little one. Doing so good that maybe I'll have to get you a cinnamon roll for breakfast." Camille giggled at my pun. "Was that all there was to the game, then?"

"Oh, no, Daddy. Not at all! Do you want to hear about the next flower?"

"Sure do." I nodded and she swiftly obliged.

"Well, now, the game got a little harder. The next picture she showed I didn't get right away." Her delicate little features showed disappointment at this failure. "It was yellow in the middle and—"

"Another daisy?" I accidentally cut her off, carried away by her former exuberance and wanting to ride to her rescue.

"No, no, no! We already did a daisy, Daddy. *Weren't you listening a minute ago?*" she chided, flipping the tables on a question she heard from me or her mother ten times a day.

It was my turn to laugh. "So sorry, hon, please continue."

"Awright. If you're ready now. *And listening.* So … the third flower. It was yellow in the middle but also had yellow petals coming out from around the middle part. Not a daisy, though, because that one has white petals," she raised her eyebrows when delivering this last sentence to make sure I understood the difference. "You talked to me about this flower once before. Said you saw them when you were a kid. You and aunties Kara and Kris liked seeing them since they were a sign of spring coming after … brrrr … winter. You know, when you were little and lived in O-hi-yo."

"You remembered me telling you about that?" Her young brain mind was like a new computer with unlimited memory. Whatever data got input into her files, was stored there forever.

"Yep, I love your stories of when you were small like me. Wish I coulda' known and played with you back then … But back to the game. I didn't know the name of that flower. Tell me, what was it?"

"They're called daffodils, Camille."

"DAFFODILS! That's it!" Her joy exploded at this epiphany.

"Honey, we should probably get you out of bed, washed up, and dressed. Then we can go pick up something for breakfast. Maybe those cinnamon pastries. We'll get Mommy one and surprise her with it," I suggested.

"Yeah, that'd be good! I like going for rides in the car with you in the morning. Saturdays are our days, aren't they? Hey— you didn't let me finish about the Flower Lady."

"Oops. I beg your pardon. Go ahead …"

"If you'll let me," she sighed, having to put up with her overzealous father. "Okay. There was one more she showed me.

This time, I sure didn't know. It was big. And it was a pretty color of pink. She said they could be white and other colors too, but pink was her favorite. Pink is the best, I think." Camille giggled again at the unplanned rhyming. "The Flower Lady said pink was the best too. And this flower was on top of a long green branch." She meant stem not branch, but hadn't learned that word yet.

Taking a moment so as not to interrupt again, I painted a mental picture from her description. "What you're describing sounds like a lilly."

"Wow—you're smart. That's what it was!" Seeing her glow with pride at my success was a charming snapshot in time I tucked away. All of a sudden, her tiny brow furrowed. "Wait a minute. The Flower Lady told me that if I figured out the name of the last one, I'd know her name too. She said her mother named her after it. Neat, huh?"

"Yes. Sometimes parents do that: name their kids after beautiful things. My own grandma got her name like that. She was a 'Lilly.' It suited her, because, boy, did she love flowers. She grew all kinds in a garden and used them to make things with them for everyone she liked." Then I added, more for myself than my daughter, "I loved her a lot. I wish you could have met her. She would have LOVED you."

"Why can't I meet her, *for real*?" Cami was indignant.

"Oh, darling, she died way before you were born."

"Aww. That's not fair, Daddy," she pouted. Rebounding, she asked, "Why did you love her so much, though?"

"For a ton of reasons which would take all morning to tell. But one thing was extra special, something she did that no one else ever did, not even my own mommy. It made me feel safe when I was small and scared of the night. No one else took such good care of me at bedtime."

"That's a nice story, Daddy. So the Flower Lady was your gramma? I'm glad I got to meet her."

"Cam, you're so cute but why would you think the Flower Lady and my grandma were the same person? Because they both liked flowers? That's just a coincidence."

"Uh-uh, Daddy. It wasn't that word you just said, cone-za ... It was her, all right. That's why I said you knew the Flower Lady. She told me she *knew you*. Only I didn't get 'til now that Flower Lady's real name was Lilly. And she was your gramma."

Not wanting to spoil Cami's fantasy, I tried to let her down easy through more explaining. "It's not a rare name. Why are you so sure she was my grandmother?"

"Well, that's the secret part I didn't want to tell at first. The Flower Lady, oh, Lilly, said it would be a nice surprise. Wait a second. Is now when I'm supposed to tell you the secret?" Camille crinkled her nose as she deliberated.

I prodded. "I'm sure she wouldn't mind you sharing the secret part. After all, I'm your daddy and we talk about everything."

"Yes! You're right about that. We talk every day, don't we? Okay. Here it is. She said she loved *singing to you* when you were little as much as you loved hearing her sing! Especially your favorite—the bird song."

Sweet Lord. How on earth? Camille became privy to a kindness that Lilly alone had shown me. It was so far back in time there was never a reason to tell anyone about it, including either of my girls. Yet not only did my daughter know the special thing was singing, but she named the song itself. It was the century-old "Momma's Gonna Buy You a Mockingbird" lullaby that Grams used to serenade me. You didn't forget those tender acts from childhood, especially when they came from a place of pure love.

"Camille, that is crazy cool that you learned about the secret thing between me and my grandmother. Can I ask you a favor, though?"

"Always. I'll do anything for you. What's the favor?"

"Don't tell anyone else about the singing or the bird song, okay? It's kind of private. Do you understand?"

"Not even Mommy gets to know?" She frowned in disapproval.

"Tell you what, if Mommy ever asks, you may tell her. Or if it somehow slips out when you and she are talking, I won't mind. Deal?"

Camille lit up at the prospect of everything being above-board among the three of us. "Deal!"

We sealed our bargain with another hug. Just like that, her four-year-old mind raced ahead to a more essential need. "Hey, *I'm hungry*! Can we go get those rolls at Dunkin' now?"

Wherever my grandmother was, she didn't stop caring about me or my young family. From some other place, she affirmed that the love she once poured into me hadn't waned in the least. Our bond was very much alive. Only now she extended it to Camille, who filled my own heart with the same measure of affection Grams carried for me.

* * *

Lilly wasn't the only relative who visited Camille. So did my father. And Mia. I wasn't home to witness these episodes but Alli filled me in afterward. The details supplied by Camille were incredible in themselves, as well as irrefutable. They included quirky phrases, affectations, or poses unique to these departed relatives our preschooler never had a chance to observe.

Intercessions such as these were woven into the fabric of

our family life. Fantastic as they might be treated outside our household, we grew accustomed to them. The door which opened for me decades ago hadn't closed. On the contrary, it opened wider in an invitation to my wife and my young daughter.

Alli and I talked about why this might be happening.

"The people we loved most who are gone are showing us that they're still near. That they care. Also, that they're still involved in our lives."

"It looks that way," I agreed. Alli's view on this situation interested me so I asked, "Why do *you* think?"

"I think they want us to see they share our love for Camille, the person who's become the center of our lives. The child who we give every ounce of love and scrap of energy we have," Alli sighed, "matters as much to them. Our happiness is theirs." Her usual economy with words made this modest speech meaningful.

Silence fell as we contemplated the probabilities. A few minutes later, it was her turn. "What are you thinking about now?"

"About how it is that Cam obviously sees and communicates with them. She *isn't* lying. She doesn't even know how to lie yet. The stuff she says about them, the expressions of theirs that she borrows when talking to us, even the mannerisms she uses while talking about them are uncanny. Did you see how she stood when she told you the Flower Lady story later on? Straight back, chin up, and arms behind her back with her right arm holding her left wrist. She was an exact, miniature replica of Lilly in speaking stance. Right down to the way she rocked a little while she spoke."

Alli laughed. "Oh my gosh, you are so, so right. It *was* your Grams standing there in front of us!" We chuckled at the assorted memories of Lilly giving us kindly lectures on different occasions. After enjoying them a spell, Alli posed a question. "Why do you think Cam can connect to them so well?"

"You mean compared to everyone else, other than me and you?"

"Yeah. Why her?"

I'd been wondering about this for a while and put together a hypothesis. "If you're searching for a definitive answer, I don't have one. What I do know is that there's more mystery than clarity in the hows or whys. In Cam's case, though, I have a theory. I suspect it's because not too long ago she was still *in* heaven. Since she hasn't been here with us all that long, her spiritual circuits are still linked up with her former home. Almost as strongly as her new home on Earth."

"Also, remember something else: 'time is different' over there, right? Or so they keep telling us. Maybe for Camille, so fresh in this world, she doesn't know there's an actual separation between theirs and ours. She sees and plays and talks to them just like she did *only a little while ago* in her four-year-old mind, although it was, literally, before she was born."

"Man, is that intense." Alli acquiesced. "It's tough to get your arms around it, isn't it? All that has happened ..."

"Or still *will* happen ..."

"Don't say that! It'll take years for me to process these things. Maybe you've gotten used to it, but I'm not looking for any more mystical events to cope with."

Alli grinned while nipping my prediction in the bud. Her sparkling eyes indicated that she found these experiences as transcendent as I did. Only she preferred them in smaller doses. I didn't blame her.

* * *

Reluctant light from late afternoon trickled in through the

panoramic windows. My appointments were finished for the day. There was a congratulatory speech to deliver at the senior scholarship banquet later in the evening, but it was hours away. Perched on a cushioned chair behind a mahogany desk, a wall lined with floor-to-ceiling bookshelves, and pampered with a private bathroom at the far end of this room, I soaked it in. This was the office template for an executive at one of the largest public universities in the country. Sheer luck or blessings from heaven, my ship had come in. Given the twisted turn of events that deposited me here, it had to be a little help from above.

I had been fired from my former job. *Not renewed* is what they technically called it. My sin? Having been hired three years prior by the previous president. All of us on her team were tainted because of association with her. This was my crime, anyway, in the eyes of our new leader. And so, I must be purged. Even the supervisor who hated me for my happy home life got the axe not long after delightfully terminating me. Poor man, he fancied that doing this dirty work would prove his allegiance to the incoming president and save him. It didn't. One day the executioner, the next day the executed—it was always the pattern when regimes changed. In this regard, college presidents were as ruthless as the khans, napoleons, and ceasars in history books.

In my situation, Providence made itself felt through paradoxes. It took a termination for me to land this prestigious position. Bizarre changes of fortune, professionally speaking, had always been my normal. In fact, it took a quarter of a century on a winding, potholed road with more sinister bosses than benevolent ones. If people only knew how corrupt some of these scholars really were. Behind the polished exteriors, their nonpublic behaviors could be appalling. Amoral, narcissistic, abusive, avaricious, manipulative—these traits were pervasive, and I had witnessed much worse. Periodically, they tried to lure me into their orbit with grand titles or eye-popping bonuses, but I would decline. Knowing the rejection made me an instant enemy, I always moved on to the next job before they did permanent damage to me or my family.

Gratefully, at rare intervals, this dismal trend was interrupted by two excellent bosses, both of whom happened to be women. They appointed me to important committees, head special projects, and mentored me with sound career advice over business lunches. I had miles to go before becoming as accomplished, but we bonded over shared ideals—telling the truth whether popular or not, treating everyone with dignity, advocating for the disadvantaged—and doing our jobs well, even if it meant cutting into time at home. With their backing, as well as a legion of decent people in the middle ranks of the academy, I managed to thrive. Now, following a national search, I had been selected for my new position at this exalted institution.

When I first broke the news to Alli, she didn't react as expected. "You mean we'll have to move away from Ohio, the Midwest, and our families if you take this job?" There was no joy, but plenty of accusation.

"Sweetheart, they won't let me serve as vice president from here. We'll need to live in Colorado. It's a gorgeous place. Wait until you see it, experience the climate, and slip into their outdoorsy lifestyle. I'm sure you and Camille will love it once we settle in."

She was having none of my chamber of commerce speech. "Yeah, but we'll have to leave everything we know and love behind."

Conflicted myself, I countered, "True, but Ohio will always be home. It's just a three-hour flight." Or a two and a half-day drive across a continent with a kindergartner, a fact I didn't rush to volunteer. "I know it's a gamble, but one I'm sure will pay off. 'Sides, it doesn't have to be forever. I'll have other opportunities in the future. Some of them will be back here."

Unselfish person that she was, Alli stopped herself from raining any further on my parade. We'd been together, my sixth sense informed me, forever. There had been so many peaks and valleys on our journey. "Never mind what I was saying. You just took me by surprise. It's all right, Tom. You *earned* this. I'm so proud. No, it isn't that far away. Cam and I will fall in love with it, I'm sure."

What she understood was that I didn't stay in higher education to chase after prestige or power. I chose university life so my own learning wouldn't end. I stuck with it for a different reason: students. At each rung up the ladder, I wielded that much more influence over campus culture. I was committed to making it less focused on self-gratification and more on self-development. And there was something in particular I wanted to do for them that no one else seemed to care about.

Approaching the summit of my own professional life, at last I possessed the power to take my students to the edge of a new and important frontier. It wouldn't be wasted.

Chapter 10
SYMMETRY

Aprivilege of my position was the choice to teach any class I wanted as long as it fell within my degree area. If none of the courses in the catalogue appealed to me, I could even create my own. With such license, my plan was to introduce students to a topic whose impact on my own life made all the difference.

After months of fine tuning, I convened my first *Contemporary Spirituality* seminar. Although it endorsed nothing controversial, it didn't take long to hear rumblings from fellow faculty. I had ventured into academic No Man's Land by basing my class on the premise that life had a spiritual dimension to it. Given academia's hive mentality in adhering to the standard model of research and spurning anything not measurable by it, the grumbling came as no surprise.

Although we no longer worked at the same college, I phoned my old friend Rodney. I hoped to learn about his latest book, which was getting good reviews, as well as share news of my own new project. While supportive, he nonetheless made a blunt prediction.

"Even in free-thinking Colorado, I doubt your colleagues will be pleased, Thomas. They detest anything that goes against scholarly writ. But you are a force to be reckoned with in your own right, now. Thus, you may prevail. Do you see the irony here? Until a hundred years ago, every human culture on Earth whether Stone Age or post-industrial embraced some concept of a Supreme Being, afterlife, and universe order. Only four generations removed, holding such views are, forgive the use of this term, *sacrilegious*."

Once more, his opinion was penetrating. "You're as insightful as always. To be sure, there'll be more than a few who object to what I'm doing. Only this time around it *is* different. I reached a place where I'm not afraid to teach truthfully and fearlessly. Let the chips fall where they may."

"Ah, that's my man of chivalry. *Bon voyage.* Circle back to me in a few months. I'll be awaiting word on how you fare ..."

* * *

The first semester, eighteen students enrolled. The second term, it drew forty-seven. By its third run, the class generated enough buzz that a wait list had to be established. Its appeal spoke as much to the psychological needs, or might it be *spiritual longing*, of students as much as its outside-the-mainstream content. Developmentally, they fell squarely in the middle of an intensely searching phase of life. Apart from a major field of study, so many were looking for a worthy cause or creed to anchor themselves to, something which would give their present meaning and future a purpose.

Class discussions revolved around the legitimacy of personal experience in spirituality. Choosing teaser topics which required participants to examine their views as well as prompt lively debate, I led them to ponder questions untouched in other classes. An example: debating the authenticity of a famous Christian relic, the Shroud of Turin. Between conflicting scientific data, portions of which supported both camps in this argument, was it the actual burial cloth of Christ? Or simply a brilliant medieval forgery? Warmed up with such teaser topics, it opened the gate to deeper reflections.

I challenged students to search their own histories. Were there strange or unusual moments, events, or encounters in their lives that they sensed had a higher meaning? Unexpectedly, I found that many already had brushes with a world they characterized as *strange, surreal, alternative*, and yet, regardless of the descriptor used, still overwhelmingly positive and uplifting.

Shyly at first, but gaining confidence as others paid close attention or asked questions, they opened up. One mentioned a time she felt terribly alone, at the end of her rope, only to hear the voice of her departed mother assuring her she was loved and things would get better. Several others spoke of aha moments they had which arose during chance interactions with offbeat strangers who entered the scene, gave unsolicited counsel on a deeply private matter troubling them, and then exited as enigmatically as they appeared. All told, there were as many varieties of experiences as students willing to talk about them.

For me, it was rewarding to achieve my goal of creating a forum where students didn't have to feel inhibited. It wasn't just emotional safety which let them lower their screens, but a pent-up desire to talk about the most important moments in their lives with those who might listen rather than judge. Like I had long ago, they found it was easier to avoid any mention of these matters after being stung by the condescension of others they trusted.

The most astounding disclosure came from someone who survived a horrible automobile accident. A friend, the driver, had died at the scene, while he lay trapped in the passenger seat, unconscious. Yet the skill with which he described going in and out of his body during the two hours it took first responders to extract him held the entire auditorium spellbound. Floating a few feet above the wrecked car, he painted a detailed picture of how his rescuers operated a machine to peel away the metal roof and how weird it felt seeing himself pinned inside. This student had a sudden, uncanny ability to hear what the rescue crew was thinking. The technicians seemed to be split as to his survival or not, which struck him as funny since he said that he felt wonderful out of his body. During this time, his spirit floated over to the curb where he read "L.S. loves T.M." etched into a section of the cement. Shortly afterward, he lost consciousness, awaking days later in the intensive care unit.

It wasn't until months afterward that he recovered sufficiently to return to the accident site. He admitted to not being very religious, but thought it would be a proper way to honor his friend. Parking alongside the curb where a makeshift memorial was erected, he got out to see the mementos other mourners had left. When a gust of wind pushed some of the flower bouquets and handwritten notes off from the curb, he was stunned to see the "L.S. loves T.M." precisely where he remembered it.

A girl in the front row of the class asked him why this came as a surprise when he already told us about the lover's inscription. The young man reminded her that he hadn't been conscious from the moment of collision until several days later. So, unless he *really was* out of his body, how could he have known the inscription was there?

In conclusion, the student stressed that in spite of everything—

wreckage, blood, trauma—he never felt afraid. Quite the opposite, he chose the term "comforting" when a fellow student pressed for what his main takeaway was from the event. He confessed that this sensation came from some other *force* also present and which gave him peace. Mind-bending as his tale was, at least half the seminar seemed to be processing what they heard. This was evident from the pensive faces and whispering between students.

Before adjourning, I polled the class to see if others who had not yet spoken had experiences similar to the intrepid volunteers who spoke about theirs. Maybe they were simply caught up in the moment, but another cluster of hands rose into the air. A willingness to weigh fairly what they heard and not rush to dismiss differentiated students from their professors.

If faculty often lectured students on the importance of open-mindedness, they abandoned it themselves long ago. For those with so many letters signifying advanced degrees on their business cards, this world held no mystery. We were simply here. Nature was indifferent to us or our circumstances. The whole of life on this planet was the accidental result of amino acids mixing in the primordial soup. Students weren't as jaded. Hope still flickered within. Young as they were, something whispered that a greater design lay behind the universe. And maybe they had a part to play.

I watched how much they needed to believe. In whatever way I could counteract the existential outlook which dominated university culture, I was committed to. At least some others felt the same. Because my seminar drew large numbers for as long as I served at this institution.

* * *

"Excuse me, Dr. Connor?" A gentle baritone interrupted my reading of a poetry book I had studied in my undergraduate days. Each fall, our library updated its collections and organized a sale of outdated volumes. My nostalgia for this one made me purchase it on the way here. Of course, taking twenty minutes for a caffeine fix at our frenetic Starbucks didn't give much shelter from prying eyes, so I only had myself to blame for the intrusion.

"Yes?" Lifting my nose out of the book, I beheld a dark-haired student standing near my table.

"Sorry for the interruption. I thought it was you. You might not remember me, but I took your seminar last semester." The hopeful expression hinted that he wanted my recognition to proceed. How could I forget? It was the student who mesmerized the class with the story of his car accident and out-of-body episode.

"Oh, yes. I certainly do remember you. How could I forget your extraordinary account? It took a ton of courage to share something so personal. Not many would. Thanks for being so brave."

"Truth be told, I'd never had the guts to do it if it hadn't been for you."

"Me? How so?"

"Because you created a place to talk about things like that without being laughed at, mocked, or told we were nuts. Which I'm pretty sure is the reaction I'd have gotten from other professors, only more polished, so they didn't totally humiliate me." He paused, as if his mind turned in another direction. "Until your class, I didn't tell anyone about what I went through. Only my girlfriend. Way, way after the fact. That didn't go so well."

"She didn't believe you, you mean?"

"No ... she most definitely didn't. Even after I took her to where it happened and showed her the couple's initials scratched into the cement curb. She told me it was too spooky. To drop the whole thing. Then guess what happened? She was 'busy' the next few times I texted her to meet up. Apart from commenting on each other's Instagram posts, we haven't met up for two weeks. Also, I noticed most of the photos of us together have been deleted from her site. It's like I became a social leper. So, I'd say it isn't looking too good."

"I'm sure she'll come around. You probably just knocked her off balance. People don't deal well with things beyond their immediate understanding."

The look on his face showed that he wasn't buying my optimistic prediction. Inside, I knew that he was right about the girl being frightened and pulling away. People struggled mightily with anything that touched on their mortality. Considering the terror many felt about dying, a possibility that death might be just a transition rather than an ending ought to be of immense comfort. Yet it wasn't, so deep was the fear.

"By the way, your name is Juan, right?"

"Good memory. Yes. Juan Morales."

I extended my hand and with a firm grip, he shook it. "Glad to officially make your acquaintance. Call me Tom."

"*Vice President for Student Life* Connor," he corrected me.

"Not necessary. We're just two people talking about a fascinating subject. There aren't many of us this bold, as you've already learned." He grinned at my compliment, but it gave way to a serious expression.

"There's something I wanted to ask you ever since the seminar. It didn't feel right in that setting. Plus, we ran out of time. Everyone had to rush off to other things, including you. I wasn't sure about how or even if to reach you. A sophomore making an appointment with someone at your level is intimidating. Although you seemed pretty chill. Never thought I'd run into just the guy I wanted to see at, of all places, our crowded campus coffee shop. Since I did, though, can I ask you a question which has nagged at me since class?"

"Ask away. Only before you do, know that you're exactly the kind of appointment I look for on my calendar." Students provided a welcome relief from the parade of dull committee meetings and droning of speeches, each trying to outdo the one before it, which dominated them. "Now, go ahead with what you need to ask."

"It's sort of private," he said, testing to see if I was receptive to go where he wanted to take me. "*Really* private," he clarified.

"Fine. Please, ask away."

"During the class, you referenced a friend of yours having a brush with a different reality as a child. You said it happened when he dove in the deep end of a swimming pool, couldn't really swim, and almost drowned." It was refreshing to hear a student describe accurately what I said in class. It showed that I conveyed something worth remembering. Juan continued. "You talked about *him* having the early stages of a near-death experience, right?"

"That phrase hadn't been coined at the time of his brush. Also, when it did occur, he was too young to know that's what it was. No matter, though, your recollection is spot on. Keep going." Two of my staff members strolled by, also enjoying the crisp autumn air. We waved at each other. Juan sipped his coffee, letting me complete this transaction, then picked up where he left off.

"So I'm right in the sequence of events so far? The last thing you mentioned was your friend feeling sure someone else was there looking over, caring, for him. You stopped with the story there."

"All true. So what's your question?"

"I have two, actually. First, there was a lot more detail in this experience that you left out, wasn't there?"

"True, again. There *was* quite a bit more. It didn't seem relevant, however, since I only wanted to spark a class discussion by modeling the way to show the rest of you it was safe to follow me into a socially taboo area. A summary version of my friend's experience seemed enough to do this job."

"I thought so." Still, Juan wasn't content. Next came his actual concern.

"So why didn't you tell everyone that it was *you* all this happened to? That would have made it even more powerful." So, his second sight circuits had been activated too. I wondered if the ability arrived after surviving his own near-death experience.

"Juan, can you read anyone or does it just come and go, without you controlling it?" He blushed when I upped the ante for his psychic penetration into my mind. He assumed it was payback for outing my secret. I was only curious, though, not perturbed. He lowered his voice to a whisper and answered.

"It's there … sometimes. But normally, it's like the switch is turned off. I don't seem to be able to use it whenever I want. It flips on whenever *it* wants. Over time, I kind of figured out that it was in me all along, just dormant or something. The first time it kicked on and I started hearing people was when I was in the hospital."

"Makes sense. It's the same with me. It just clicks on sometimes. Which is how I know that it was supposed to be *you* driving the night of your accident instead of your friend. Those million what-ifs haunt you. Don't let them. There is no blame to be had here." Juan didn't act surprised that I turned the tables on him. Probably because he already knew we carried the same strange mark.

"You learn to live with this ability. But let's get back to your question. Why didn't I claim the experience as my own? I suppose because, to this day, a lot of it still feels too intimate for me to divulge. I wasn't comfortable saying any more in class than I did. I trust you can respect this."

"Yeah, I can." Juan wanted much more but was polite enough not to insist on it.

"Now then … what was your second question?"

"Okay. Only don't laugh." I promised him I wouldn't.

"Did you hear the music?" He trembled in anticipation of my response.

When I didn't answer in the affirmative, his face registered disappointment. "No. I didn't notice anything musical in my encounter."

This was not a lie. During my time with Lizabeth when I was eight, there was no background sound. On the other hand, I clearly heard a hum resonating through the scene where my father and I met to bid farewell. This humming permeated everything there, but I couldn't call it a melody. What I heard seemed prayerful, a soft if pervasive chorus of praise coming from every speck of matter. Still, I hesitated to describe it to Juan. Some things, especially those related to me and my father, remained too precious.

"I guarantee that if you heard it, you'd never forget," Juan declared. "I call it the 'music of heaven.' It's soothing and uplifting at the same time. It almost *holds* me. With warmth, with affection. Sounds crazy, I know. But it really does. Even now, three years after Carlos died in the wreck, it will come to me. At night, when I'm totally worn out or depressed or missing him. After a while of listening to it, I feel good again." You had to experience them to truly know the impact of these otherworldly gifts.

Juan craved my support. "I don't doubt your ongoing contact with this higher realm. After venturing into it myself, I believe you. Want some advice? Don't ever, ever question what took place during the event or in its aftermath. I'm convinced this parallel reality is more real than what's around us this very minute. If you choose not to talk of it to others, who could blame you? We both know the result." I sighed, reflecting on the reactions I got the few times I put out the slightest feelers on my own mystical interludes.

"However, don't second guess what you know in your heart. Even if they ..." I made a sweeping motion past the chattering line of customers at the counter, pairs sitting at nearby tables, and farther away, passersby on their way to class, "... haven't been fortunate to see it too."

Juan studied my face. "Thanks a million, Dr. C.," he said, using the nickname our university newspaper bestowed upon me. "Hearing this from you means the world to me."

"My pleasure. Feel free to drop by my office any time to continue our conversation. You're always safe with me regarding this subject. We're a small club. But one with an unbreakable bond."

"Us against them?" he asked with a smile.

"I wouldn't put it that way. More like 'us trying to reach them.'" We shook hands. Seconds later, Juan joined a line of students leaving the crowded patio.

I remembered my iced tea and book of verse. Returning to it, I read again the sentence where I had been, then turned the page. There, my eyes fell upon this poet's celebrated line: Humankind cannot bear too much reality. Call it synchronicity, because it seemed to reinforce what Juan and I, two outliers, had to contend with. Humankind cannot bear too much *meta*-reality either, I thought to myself.

Although we didn't speak again, our paths crossed periodically. Other students—Kaitlyn, Jace, Jordan, Akila, and more—with their own metaphysical experiences followed. Most just ached to hear they weren't delusional. Enough persistence of spiritual memory lingered in them to indicate otherwise. If my class addressed this longing, it was a modest repayment for what this other side had shown me.

Let the critics, none of them students, say what they wanted. It no longer fazed me.

CHAPTER 11
HORIZONS

"How's your glass? Care for more of this so-so wine?" Dinner was done and the table cleared. It was just Alli and me in the tranquility of early evening. Behind our house, elongated shadows sprawled over an emerald lawn. A squirrel rummaged through the blades of grass in search of his supper. Wine glasses in hand, we loitered around the kitchen island.

"Nah, I'm good with what I have. What's wrong with it, by the way?" No expert on wine, I didn't follow the critique. My preference would've been a beer so cold it contained slivers of ice. Alli teased that my tastes mirrored our place of origin. "I can take you out of the Midwest, but not the Midwest out of you," she joked. The wine came as a housewarming gift from neighbors on our new street. I felt a bit sad that I couldn't appreciate it as they intended.

Our time out West had been good. We enjoyed the climate, mountains, and its live-and-let-live attitude. Unfortunately, as a poet mused, nothing gold can stay. In my case, the dream job—a presidency—opened up at a foundation back East. If I pursued it, we had to make another major move. It would also mean the end of my twenty-six years in higher education. Bittersweet as it could have been, I didn't hesitate. As a teacher who really cared about students, the collection of mementos from them accumulating in my office showed I made a difference. Truth be told, I was finished with the darker side of higher education. The politics and egos that warped its upper echelons eroded the love I once had for universities. Head and heart both told me it was time for my second act.

So, we returned home, or nearer to it anyhow, relocating to a stately suburb at the edge of a southern city. It was to be the next chapter in our journey, one of canopy roads and live oaks dripping Spanish moss, sultry summers, and neighbors with accents so mellifluous they beguiled you. Naturally, Alli couldn't contain her elation to be just a half-day's car ride away from family in Ohio. Everything felt fresh and new again, like we had been reborn.

Our kitchen windows were wide open. The scent of pine boughs and magnolia blossoms mingled on the breeze. Alli clinked her glass against mine. "Thanks for bringing us closer to home. I know it's only been a month for you on the new job. And another jump into the unknown. I hope this one turns out to be your best ever. You deserve it."

"I hope so. Feels good right now. It's glorious being in the position of giving grants rather than begging for them. For the first time in my career, I might add!" I rolled my eyes at the long overdue reversal of fortune, making Alli laugh and roll her own eyes in agreement. "But you're right: any new job is always a gamble. Relocating from one side of the country to the other. Only time will tell if it was worth the risk."

"Everything worthwhile we've done has been a leap of faith. You helped me see that. When we met, I'd have been happy to stay in the neighborhood where I was born. Look at me today. The places we've lived. The people we've met. The experiences we've had. I wouldn't change them for the world. Thanks for making me unafraid." She stopped, searching for her next words. "You are the most fearless person I know, Tom. How lucky I am that you took a chance on that silly girl who ran smack into you one fine day all those years ago."

"Oh, yes ... *her*. Well, I didn't have anything better to do. Figured I might as well give her a shot." Alli opened her mouth in mock outrage and slapped me on the shoulder. "Kidding aside, it's me who ought to be thanking you. For being my partner on this exhilarating, unpredictable, and never boring ride."

A bird bath in the yard attracted a sunset crowd. We watched a covey of sparrows square off against a pair of brawny cardinals, chirping madly at each other for rights to the water. After much ado, and in spite of their bulk, the cardinals yielded to the aggressiveness of the smaller birds and flew away. A fresh wave of garden scents wafted into the room.

I remembered something. "Hey, before dinner, what did Camille say when she phoned? About the roommate? Are they getting along?" Even when she wasn't with us, Cami still arose as the centerpiece of many conversations.

"So far, so good. Her roomie is young too, sixteen, so about six months older than ours. Who'd have thought Cam would start college at that age? She's something else." I smiled, remembering this echoed what my father said about our girl making a splash even in his corner of heaven. We moved Camille into her dorm room this morning. It was a small college where a girl her age could safely stretch her wings. Not that she needed much monitoring. Hers was an old soul.

Two days prior, she and I were reminiscing about her

childhood and our favorite memories. Her list, of course, looked different from mine. Cam's consisted of all her "firsts": trip to the beach, performance at a ballet recital, smiling at the entrance to a nursing home after she delivered her hand-painted Christmas cards, and the like. We laughed at how well she negotiated those rites of passage, publicly, while her mother and I privately weathered her considerable jitters beforehand. Then it was my turn. I asked if she ever thought about the Flower Lady or those other interactions she had with relatives she never met. Making a valiant effort to let me down easy, she said, sorry, Dad, but, no, I don't remember them anymore. No problem, they happened a long time ago, I assured her.

Regardless, their legacy lived on. When we saw the level-headed teen that she became and the smart choices she made in these chaotic times, we liked to believe that Lilly, Mia, or my father watched over her and every now and then whispered sage advice in her ear. We had seen how effortlessly their love spread over generations.

"She's going to be okay," Alli was saying, bringing me back to kitchen. "With her strong personality and independent streak, no one will push her to do anything she doesn't want to."

"Isn't that an understatement?!" We laughed again, then our conversation halted as we sipped wine and mentally doted on our daughter.

I came back to my wife. While she watched the victorious sparrows splashing in their prize, I marveled at how lucky I was to be with her. After this much time, I still got butterflies thinking about our reunion when we weren't together.

"I suppose it's just us now." I sighed. A curtain of sadness dropped down. Like that, we were suddenly empty nesters. It was status thrust upon us that we weren't ready to embrace.

Unsurprisingly, wisdom spilled from my wife's lips.

"*It's always been just us*, Tom. From the day we met." Leave it to her to take me from wistfulness to joy in an instant.

"Yeah. It has." I reached for her hand and squeezed her slender fingers. "Well, *almost*," I corrected, with a grin.

"Ahh, yes, of course … *them*. The heaven-sent people. Guess I'm okay with sharing you." She smiled back with those arresting eyes. I fell in love again for the millionth time.

"Are you so sure that they're coming from heaven?" Not that I thought differently, but I was interested in hearing Alli's view. "Maybe it's just another dimension we can't understand. Doesn't modern physics speculate that there are up to eleven other universes or something?

"I'm no expert. But heaven would have to be another universe or dimension. It sure isn't this one, is it? Back to your question though: do I think that's where they're coming from? If not, where else? Especially seeing how they've *changed*. I don't mean your Lizabeth or the mystery girl on campus who said God loved you. They must have been … I don't know … even higher beings. But Mia, your dad, and Grams, as actual people, seemed somehow … purer. Their personalities were the same, but whatever good traits they had seemed amplified. They were all and only goodness now."

She had me there. In life, each of them showed the same imperfections as the rest of us. Yet these weren't in evidence anymore. They had inched closer to perfect. Alli must be right, heaven had to account for the difference.

Another lull paused the conversation. Each of us imagining what it must be like there and realizing in spite of everything, that it would remain a mystery until it was our turn to know. After a spell, she broke the silence.

"Think you'll ever really tell anyone … about things?" Alli meant my history of interactions with this other realm. My trust in her was so complete that I told her—only recently—my entire story, from meeting Lizabeth at eight and all that followed. She said, now I get it. This explains so much about you. True to character, Alli was the one person who wouldn't judge or doubt or ridicule me. Nor did it hurt that she had been privy to a few miracles of her own.

I shrugged, unwilling to rekindle the debate in myself over this question and spoil the pleasant mood. Telling it all to the love of my life was one thing. The idea of everyone else still put a knot in my stomach. "Even if I did, no one would believe me."

Her eyes clouded at my observation. There was sorrow in them. "Strange, isn't it? People hear a hundred lies a day, from television, the internet, people they know, and don't question them. But tell them a story with one important truth, and no one's likely to believe it. Talk about ironic."

"Amen to that. Mention the word 'spiritual' in this day and age and people peg you as a crackpot. Describe full-on immersion experiences and they flee as if you're a danger to society."

Unsolicited, Alli gently took my wine glass and set it on the counter. She opened the freezer, pulled out a bottle of beer tucked away in the back, still unfrozen. Then she handed it to me and winked. What a woman.

"Still, it doesn't mean that I should never try." I considered the Tall Man's prophecy. And what Mia, Lilly, and my father probably expected of me but were gracious enough not to say.

"For what it's worth, I think you should." She came closer and leaned her head against my chest. I took hold of her shoulder.

"Hey. Weren't you going to tell me about Belize, when you went last month on that Habitat for Humanity project your foundation funded? Said you saw something amazing there you've never seen before. You promised to tell, remember?"

Oh yes. For those three days, streaming from everything— Light.

Not tonight. "It can wait. With our daughter gone and it being just us, this evening is all ours." We took long draws from our drinks and watched the sparrows splashing outside.

POSTSCRIPT

There's more to this story that I didn't include. Borrowing a phrase from my Carolina neighbors, let's just "… sit with things ah-while." A lot can happen when you are still, calm, and listening.

I still don't know why it was me who got to see these things. Anyone else is probably more deserving. Although I live by the Golden Rule, *saintly* would not be among the first words coming to mind when family or friends describe me. Just ask Alli, and once she stops laughing, she's sure to set you straight. I wouldn't want it any other way. I like myself better for having these shortcomings. Striving to improve gives me something worthwhile to focus on. We're all works in progress, after all.

One thing I am sure of, though, is that there are no real borders between what is here and what comes next. Realities converge when it's time for a transcendent moment to move you forward. Messengers are every place. All you need to do is tune in and they will speak to you.

They still speak to me, at unexpected times and in mundane situations. Take the taciturn teenager who aided me and my wife at the side of a busy freeway when our car broke down. Dozens of other vehicles roared by in clouds of exhaust, but not his.

Picking us up, he didn't drop us at the closest gas station but on our doorstep *eighty miles* away. When Alli asked why he stopped in the first place, this overgrown kid said any couple holding hands as they walked along the shoulder of a filthy highway must be decent enough folk. Before parting ways, she wrote down his address and later mailed him a check for his trouble. The envelope came back to us, stamped: Return to Sender, Address Unknown. On and on it goes.

There's nothing remarkable about me or Alli or my family. We're as average as they come. We talk, agree, and argue. If feelings get hurt, the offender apologizes and promises to try harder. The next day arrives. We have a fresh chance to get it right—the universe is generous in this regard. Whether we rise to the occasion or the world drags us down and tempers flare again, there's a consolation prize. It's the gift of knowing our love for each other will not falter. It persists, even after we leave here. Those we loved who are already over there have proven it.

Whatever you choose to call the next world, and I'm good with *heaven*, it isn't distant. It is here, now, overlapping with the reality in which we live. There's also a time before this one, as well as a time after this. All their secrets will eventually be revealed.

With as much road behind me in the rearview mirror as still lay ahead, it's time for me to speak up. Who am I to say no to heaven?

Call me Jonah.

ABOUT THE AUTHOR

W ill Alexander is a teacher, scholar, and college president. He served in leadership roles at many renowned American universities. After decades in higher education, he refocused on his lifelong passion—writing about the transcendent moments that all of us have experienced and how they impact the course of our lives.

Other Books by Ozark Mountain Publishing, Inc.

Dolores Cannon
A Soul Remembers Hiroshima
Between Death and Life
Conversations with Nostradamus,
    Volume I, II, III
The Convoluted Universe -Book One,
    Two, Three, Four, Five
The Custodians
Five Lives Remembered
Horns of the Goddess
Jesus and the Essenes
Keepers of the Garden
Legacy from the Stars
The Legend of Starcrash
The Search for Hidden Sacred
    Knowledge
They Walked with Jesus
The Three Waves of Volunteers and the
    New Earth
A Very Special Friend
Aron Abrahamsen
Holiday in Heaven
James Ream Adams
Little Steps
Justine Alessi & M. E. McMillan
Rebirth of the Oracle
Kathryn Andries
Time: The Second Secret
Will Alexander
Call Me Jonah
Cat Baldwin
Divine Gifts of Healing
The Forgiveness Workshop
Penny Barron
The Oracle of UR
P.E. Berg & Amanda Hemmingsen
The Birthmark Scar
Dan Bird
Finding Your Way in the Spiritual Age
Waking Up in the Spiritual Age
Julia Cannon
Soul Speak – The Language of Your
    Body
Jack Cauley
Journey for Life
Ronald Chapman
Seeing True
Jack Churchward
Lifting the Veil on the Lost
    Continent of Mu

The Stone Tablets of Mu
Carolyn Greer Daly
Opening to Fullness of Spirit
Patrick De Haan
The Alien Handbook
Paulinne Delcour-Min
Divine Fire
Holly Ice
Spiritual Gold
Anthony DeNino
The Power of Giving and Gratitude
Joanne DiMaggio
Edgar Cayce and the Unfulfilled
    Destiny of Thomas Jefferson
    Reborn
Paul Fisher
Like a River to the Sea
Anita Holmes
Twidders
Aaron Hoopes
Reconnecting to the Earth
Edin Huskovic
God is a Woman
Patricia Irvine
In Light and In Shade
Kevin Killen
Ghosts and Me
Susan Linville
Blessings from Agnes
Donna Lynn
From Fear to Love
Curt Melliger
Heaven Here on Earth
Where the Weeds Grow
Henry Michaelson
And Jesus Said – A Conversation
Andy Myers
Not Your Average Angel Book
Holly Nadler
The Hobo Diaries
Guy Needler
The Anne Dialogues
Avoiding Karma
Beyond the Source – Book 1, Book 2
The Curators
The History of God
The OM
The Origin Speaks

For more information about any of the above titles, soon to be released titles,
or other items in our catalog, write, phone or visit our website:
PO Box 754, Huntsville, AR 72740|479-738-2348/800-935-0045|www.ozarkmt.com

Other Books by Ozark Mountain Publishing, Inc.

Psycho Spiritual Healing
James Nussbaumer
And Then I Knew My Abundance
Each of You
Living Your Dram, Not Someone Else's
The Master of Everything
Mastering Your Own Spiritual Freedom
Sherry O'Brian
Peaks and Valley's
Gabrielle Orr
Akashic Records: One True Love
Let Miracles Happen
Nikki Pattillo
Children of the Stars
A Golden Compass
Victoria Pendragon
Being In A Body
Sleep Magic
The Sleeping Phoenix
Alexander Quinn
Starseeds What's It All About
Debra Rayburn
Let's Get Natural with Herbs
Charmian Redwood
A New Earth Rising
Coming Home to Lemuria
Richard Rowe
Exploring the Divine Library
Imagining the Unimaginable
Garnet Schulhauser
Dance of Eternal Rapture
Dance of Heavenly Bliss
Dancing Forever with Spirit
Dancing on a Stamp
Dancing with Angels in Heaven
Annie Stillwater Gray
The Dawn Book
Education of a Guardian Angel
Joys of a Guardian Angel
Work of a Guardian Angel
Manuella Stoerzer
Headless Chicken

Blair Styra
Don't Change the Channel
Who Catharted
Natalie Sudman
Application of Impossible Things
L.R. Sumpter
Judy's Story
The Old is New
We Are the Creators
Artur Tradevosyan
Croton
Croton II
Jim Thomas
Tales from the Trance
Jolene and Jason Tierney
A Quest of Transcendence
Paul Travers
Dancing with the Mountains
Nicholas Vesey
Living the Life-Force
Dennis Wheatley/ Maria Wheatley
The Essential Dowsing Guide
Maria Wheatley
Druidic Soul Star Astrology
Sherry Wilde
The Forgotten Promise
Lyn Willmott
A Small Book of Comfort
Beyond all Boundaries Book 1
Beyond all Boundaries Book 2
Beyond all Boundaries Book 3
D. Arthur Wilson
You Selfish Bastard
Stuart Wilson & Joanna Prentis
Atlantis and the New Consciousness
Beyond Limitations
The Essenes -Children of the Light
The Magdalene Version
Power of the Magdalene
Sally Wolf
Life of a Military Psychologist

For more information about any of the above titles, soon to be released titles,
or other items in our catalog, write, phone or visit our website:
PO Box 754, Huntsville, AR 72740|479-738-2348/800-935-0045|www.ozarkmt.com